KITCHEN
TABLE

100 Quick Stir-fry Recipes

The best recipes from your favourite chefs – now in your pocket!

- Download the app now and get 40 amazing recipes. Plus you can buy more recipes at any time – 340 more tasty dishes available in 7 carefully chosen collections.

- Clearly laid out recipes let you flick between introduction, ingredients and steps - plus you can create a shopping basket and share with friends at the touch of a button!

- Fully customisable search means you will always find a great recipe.

- You can also activate our revolutionary Touch-Free mode - perfect for when your hands are a little dirty in the kitchen.

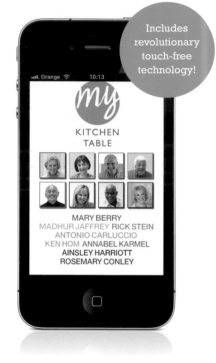

Includes revolutionary touch-free technology!

Find out more at www.mykitchentable.co.uk/app

my KITCHEN TABLE

KITCHEN
TABLE

100 Quick Stir-fry Recipes
KEN HOM

www.mykitchentable.co.uk

Welcome to  KITCHEN TABLE

Stir-fries can be the simplest, quickest and healthiest
of meals to cook, and here I have brought together
100 of my favourite recipes. I hope you enjoy cooking
them, and I wish you good health and delicious eating.

Contents

Chicken and poultry   6

Meat dishes   40

Fish and seafood   72

Vegetarian dishes   100

Pasta, rice and noodles   136

Soups, appetisers and sides   170

Index   206

Stir-fried Chicken with Grilled Peppers

As a student living in southern France, I discovered the taste of grilled or roasted peppers. Cooked over an open flame on a stove or barbecue, peppers acquire an exquisitely sweet, smoky flavour.

Step one Using tongs, hold each pepper directly over a gas flame and cook until the skin has blackened all over. If you don't have a gas stove, put them under a hot grill, turning occasionally, until blackened. Place in a plastic bag and close it tightly. When the peppers have cooled, remove from the bag and peel off the charred skin. Clean the insides and discard the seeds. Cut the peppers into strips, drizzle them with the oil and set aside.

Step two Cut the chicken into 2.5cm (1in) cubes. Mix with all the marinade ingredients in a small bowl, season with 1 teaspoon of salt, then chill for 20 minutes.

Step three If using ground nut oil to cook the chicken, heat a wok or large frying pan over a high heat and add the oil. When it is very hot, remove the wok or pan from the heat and immediately add the chicken pieces, stirring vigorously to prevent them sticking. When they turn white, after about 2 minutes, quickly drain the chicken in a stainless-steel colander set in a bowl. Discard the oil. If using water instead of oil, bring it to the boil in a pan, then remove from the heat and immediately add the chicken pieces, stirring vigorously to prevent them sticking. When the chicken pieces turn white, after about 2 minutes, quickly drain them in a colander set in a bowl. Discard the water.

Step four If you used a wok or pan, wipe it clean. Reheat it, then add the tablespoon of ground nut oil. When it is very hot, add the garlic slices and stir-fry for 2 minutes, until golden brown.

Step five Add the stock, chilli bean sauce, sugar, rice wine or sherry and soy sauce. Cook for 2 minutes, then add the cornflour and water mixture and cook for 20 seconds.

Step six Add the chicken and the roasted pepper strips and stir-fry for another 2 minutes. Serve at once.

Serves 4

4 peppers, a mixture of red, yellow and green

2 tbsp extra-virgin olive oil

450g (1lb) boneless skinless chicken breasts

300ml (½ pint) ground nut oil or water

1 tbsp ground nut oil

2 tbsp finely sliced garlic

150ml (¼ pint) home-made or good-quality bought chicken stock

2 tsp chilli bean sauce

2 tsp sugar

1½ tbsp Shaoxing rice wine or dry sherry

1 tbsp light soy sauce

1 tsp cornflour, blended with 1 tbsp water

for the marinade

1 egg white

2 tsp cornflour

salt

Shredded Chicken with Sesame Seeds

This is my version of a fragrant Sichuan dish popularly known as 'Strange Taste Chicken' because it incorporates so many flavours, being hot, spicy, sour, sweet and salty all at the same time. It is delicious served hot but I find it makes an excellent cold dish as well. I simply let it cool and serve it at room temperature.

Serves 3–4

450g (1lb) boneless skinless chicken breasts

300ml (½ pint) ground nut oil or water

1 tbsp ground nut oil

1 tbsp white sesame seeds

for the marinade

1 egg white

2 tsp cornflour

salt

for the sauce

2 tsp dark soy sauce

2 tsp Chinese black rice vinegar or cider vinegar

2 tsp chilli bean sauce

2 tsp sesame oil

2 tsp sugar

1 tbsp Shaoxing rice wine or dry sherry

1 tsp whole Sichuan peppercorns, roasted

1½ tbsp finely chopped spring onions

Step one Cut the chicken breasts into strips 7.5cm (3in) long. Mix with all the marinade ingredients in a small bowl, season with ½ teaspoon of salt and chill for about 20 minutes.

Step two If using ground nut oil to cook the chicken, heat a wok or frying pan over a high heat and then add the oil. When it is very hot, remove the wok from the heat and immediately add the chicken pieces, stirring vigorously to prevent them sticking. After about 2 minutes, when the chicken pieces turn white, quickly drain them in a stainless-steel colander set in a bowl. Discard the oil. If using water instead of oil, bring it to the boil in a pan, then remove from the heat and immediately add the chicken pieces, stirring vigorously to prevent them sticking. After about 2 minutes, when the chicken pieces turn white, quickly drain them in a colander set in a bowl. Discard the water.

Step three If you used a wok or pan, wipe it clean. Heat it until it is very hot, then add the tablespoon of oil. Immediately add the sesame seeds and stir-fry for 30 seconds or until brown.

Step four Add all the sauce ingredients and bring to the boil. Return the cooked chicken to the pan and stir-fry the mixture for another 2 minutes, coating the pieces thoroughly with the sauce and sesame seeds. Serve at once or let it cool and serve at room temperature.

Chicken with Chillies and Basil

This traditional dish, called *gai phad bai krapao*, is very easy to prepare. Although ordinary fresh basil is fine, if you can find Thai basil, its unique, pungent aroma makes the dish especially mouth-watering.

Step one Heat a wok or large frying pan until it is very hot, then add 1 tablespoon of the oil. When it is very hot, add the chicken and stir-fry over a high heat for 8 minutes, until browned all over. Using a slotted spoon, transfer the chicken to a colander or sieve to drain.

Step two Reheat the wok and add the remaining oil. Toss in the shallots and garlic and stir-fry for 3 minutes, until they are golden brown.

Step three Return the chicken to the wok and add the chilli peppers, fish sauce, dark soy sauce and sugar. Stir-fry over a high heat for 8 minutes or until the chicken is cooked through. Stir in the basil leaves and serve at once.

Serves 4

2 tbsp ground nut oil

450g (1lb) boneless skinless chicken thighs, cut into 2.5cm (1in) pieces

3 tbsp finely sliced shallots

3 tbsp chopped garlic

for the sauce

3 fresh red or green Thai chilli peppers, de-seeded and finely shredded

2 tbsp fish sauce (nam pla)

2 tsp dark soy sauce

2 tsp sugar

a large handful of basil leaves

Indonesian-style Chicken with Vegetables

This is a typically hearty, family-style stir fry that is packed full of flavour.

Serves 4–6

225g (8oz) broccoli (about 1 head)

225g (8oz) asparagus

225g (8oz) baby sweetcorn

3 tbsp ground nut oil

450g (1lb) boneless skinless chicken thighs, cut into 2.5cm (1in) pieces

2 tbsp finely sliced garlic

3 tbsp finely sliced shallots

2 large, fresh red chilli peppers, de-seeded and sliced

1 tbsp finely sliced fresh root ginger

1½ tbsp light soy sauce

2 tsp shrimp paste

2 tsp sugar

225g (8oz) button mushrooms, thinly sliced

2 tbsp home-made or good-quality bought chicken stock or water

salt and pepper

Step one Cut the stalks off the broccoli and divide the heads into small florets. Peel the stalks and thinly slice them on the diagonal. Trim the woody ends off the asparagus and then cut into 4cm (1½in) lengths.

Step two Bring a large pan of salted water to the boil and blanch the broccoli and baby sweetcorn for 3 minutes. Drain, and plunge them into cold water to stop them cooking further, then drain again.

Step three Heat a wok or large frying pan over a high heat. Add the oil and, when it is very hot and slightly smoking, add the chicken pieces and stir-fry for 5 minutes or until golden brown. Remove the chicken with a slotted spoon and leave to drain in a colander or sieve.

Step four Reheat the wok over a high heat until it is medium hot. Add the garlic, shallots, chilli peppers and ginger and stir-fry for about 2 minutes, until golden brown. Then add the soy sauce, shrimp paste, sugar, 1 teaspoon of salt and a little pepper and stir-fry for 1 minute.

Step five Now add to the wok the broccoli, corn, asparagus and mushrooms and continue to stir-fry for 3 minutes.

Step six Return the drained chicken to the wok, add the stock or water and cook over a high heat for 5 minutes or until the chicken is thoroughly cooked. Turn out onto a platter and serve at once.

Stir-fried Chicken with Black Bean Sauce

This is a favourite of many first-time diners in Chinese restaurants, and no wonder. The fragrance of fermented black bean sauce mixed with garlic and ginger is mouth-watering. It can be cooked ahead of time and reheated, and it is also delicious served cold.

Step one Put the chicken in a bowl and mix with the soy sauce, rice wine or sherry, sugar, sesame oil, cornflour and ½ teaspoon of salt.

Step two Heat a wok over a high heat, then add the oil. When it is very hot and slightly smoking, add the chicken and stir-fry for around 2 minutes.

Step three Then add the ginger, garlic, shallots, 1½ tablespoons of the spring onions, and the black beans and stir-fry for around 2 minutes.

Step four Finally, add the stock. Bring the mixture to the boil, then reduce the heat, cover and simmer for 3 minutes or until the chicken is cooked. Garnish with the remaining spring onions and serve.

Serves 4

450g (1lb) boneless skinless chicken breasts, cut into 5cm (2in) chunks

1 tbsp light soy sauce

1½ tbsp Shaoxing rice wine or dry sherry

1 tsp sugar

1 tsp sesame oil

2 tsp cornflour

2 tbsp ground nut oil

1 tbsp finely chopped fresh root ginger

1½ tbsp coarsely chopped garlic

2 tbsp finely chopped shallots

3½ tbsp finely chopped spring onions

2½ tbsp coarsely chopped salted black beans

150ml (¼ pint) home-made or good-quality bought chicken stock

salt

Spicy Chicken with Peanuts

This classic western Chinese dish is better known as *gongbao* or *kung pao* chicken. There are many versions of this recipe; this one is close to the original and is also easy to make.

Serves 4

3 tbsp ground nut oil

3 dried red chillies, split lengthways in half

450g (1lb) boneless skinless chicken breasts, cut into 2.5cm (1in) chunks

75g (3oz) roasted peanuts

for the sauce

2 tbsp home-made or good-quality bought chicken stock

2 tbsp Shaoxing rice wine or dry sherry

1 tbsp dark soy sauce

2 tsp sugar

1 tbsp coarsely chopped garlic

2 tsp finely chopped spring onions

1 tsp finely chopped fresh root ginger

2 tsp Chinese white rice vinegar or cider vinegar

2 tsp sesame oil

salt

Step one Heat a wok over a high heat. Add the oil and chillies and stir-fry for a few seconds (you may remove the chillies when they turn black or leave them in).

Step two Next add the chicken and peanuts and stir-fry for 1 minute. Remove the chicken, peanuts and chillies from the wok and drain in a colander.

Step three Put all the sauce ingredients except the sesame oil into the wok and add 1 teaspoon of salt. Bring to the boil and then turn the heat down.

Step four Return the chicken, peanuts and chillies to the wok and cook for about 3–4 minutes in the sauce, mixing well.

Step five Finally, add the sesame oil, give the mixture a good stir, remove the chillies, if you prefer, and serve immediately.

Classic Lemon Chicken

This tart sauce goes very well indeed with the flavour of chicken.

Step one Put the chicken strips in a bowl and combine with the egg white, sesame oil, cornflour and 1 teaspoon of salt. Chill for about 20 minutes.

Step two If you are using oil for 'velveting' the chicken, heat a wok until very hot and then add the oil. When it is very hot, remove the wok from the heat and immediately add the chicken, stirring vigorously to prevent it sticking. After about 2 minutes, when the chicken turns white, quickly drain it and all of the oil in a stainless-steel colander set over a bowl. Discard the oil. If using water, do the same but bring the water to the boil and put the chicken in to cook. It will take about 4 minutes to turn white in the water.

Step three If you have used a wok, wipe it clean. Heat it, then add all the sauce ingredients except the cornflour mixture and sesame oil. Bring to a boil over a high heat and then add the cornflour mixture. Simmer for 1 minute.

Step four Return the chicken strips to the wok and stir-fry long enough to coat them all with the sauce. Mix in the sesame oil, then turn onto a platter, garnish with the spring onions and serve at once.

Serves 4

450g (1lb) boneless skinless chicken breasts, cut into strips 7.5 x 1cm (3 x ½ in) thick

1 egg white

1 tsp sesame oil

2 tsp cornflour

300ml (½ pint) ground nut oil or water

2 tbsp finely chopped spring onions, to garnish

salt

for the sauce

65ml (2½ fl oz) home-made or good-quality bought chicken stock

3 tbsp fresh lemon juice

1 tbsp sugar

1 tbsp light soy sauce

1½ tbsp Shaoxing rice wine or dry sherry

1½ tbsp finely chopped garlic

1–2 tsp crushed dried red chilli

1 tsp cornflour, blended with 1 tsp water

2 tsp sesame oil

Chinese Chicken Curry

Curry blends well with chicken, especially when used Chinese-style as a light sauce that does not overpower the delicate taste of the meat.

Serves 4

450g (1lb) boneless skinless chicken breasts, cut into 2.5cm (1in) chunks

1 egg white

1 tsp sesame oil

3 tsp cornflour

300ml (½ pint) ground nut oil or water

1 tbsp ground nut oil

225g (8oz) red or green peppers, de-seeded and cut into 2.5cm (1in) pieces

1 tbsp coarsely chopped garlic

150ml (¼ pint) home-made or good-quality bought chicken stock

1½ tbsp Madras curry paste or powder

2 tsp sugar

1½ tbsp Shaoxing rice wine or dry sherry

1½ tbsp light soy sauce

1 tsp cornflour, blended with 1 tbsp water

a handful of fresh coriander leaves

salt

Step one Put the chicken pieces in a bowl with the egg white, sesame oil, 2 teaspoons of the cornflour and 1 teaspoon of salt and mix well. Chill the mixture for about 20 minutes.

Step two If you are using oil for velveting the chicken, heat a wok until very hot and then add the oil. When it is very hot, remove the wok from the heat and immediately add the chicken, stirring vigorously to prevent it sticking. After about 2 minutes, when the chicken turns white, quickly drain it and all of the oil in a stainless-steel colander set over a bowl. Discard the oil. If using water, do exactly the same but bring the water to the boil and put in the chicken to cook. It will take about 4 minutes to turn white in the water.

Step three If you have used the wok, wipe it clean. Heat it until it is very hot, then add the tablespoon of ground nut oil. When it is very hot, add the peppers and garlic and stir-fry for 2 minutes.

Step four Add the stock, curry paste or powder, sugar, rice wine or sherry, soy sauce and cornflour mixture. Cook for 2 minutes. Add the drained chicken to the wok and stir-fry for another 2 minutes, coating the chicken thoroughly with the sauce. Serve at once, garnished with the coriander leaves.

Green Chicken Curry

The richness of the coconut milk combined with green curry paste and chicken is a winning combination.

Step one Cut the chicken into 2.5cm (1in) chunks. Peel off the tough outer layers of the sticks of lemon grass, leaving the tender, whitish centre, and chop it finely.

Step two Heat a wok or large frying pan until it is very hot and add the oil. Add the green curry paste and stir-fry for 2 minutes, then add the chicken and mix until it is coated with the paste.

Step three Now add the lemon grass, shallots, garlic, galangal or ginger, lime leaves or zest, fish sauce, sugar and 1 teaspoon of salt and stir fry for another minute.

Step four Add the aubergines and pour in the coconut milk and 3 tablespoons of water. Turn the heat to low and simmer for around 15 minutes or until the chicken is cooked through. Add the coriander and basil leaves, give the mixture a good stir and serve at once.

Serves 4

450g (1lb) boneless skinless chicken thighs

2 sticks of lemon grass

1½ tbsp vegetable oil

2–3 tbsp Thai green curry paste

3 tbsp finely sliced shallots

3 tbsp coarsely chopped garlic

1 tbsp finely chopped fresh galangal or root ginger

4 kaffir lime leaves or 2 tsp shredded lime zest

1 tbsp fish sauce (nam pla)

2 tsp sugar

225g (8oz) pea aubergines, left whole, or ordinary aubergines cut into 2.5cm (1in) chunks

1 x 400ml (14fl oz) tin of coconut milk

a handful of fresh coriander leaves

a handful of fresh Thai basil leaves

salt

For Ken Hom's guide to equipment, go to www.mykitchentable.co.uk/authors/KenHom/equipment

Red Chicken Curry

Gaeng phed gai is a slightly different version of Thai chicken curry from the previous one, using red curry paste. It is just as delicious.

Serves 4

450g (1lb) boneless skinless chicken thighs

2 sticks of lemon grass

1½ tbsp vegetable oil

2–3 tbsp Thai red curry paste

225g (8oz) small potatoes, peeled

3 tbsp finely sliced shallots

3 tbsp coarsely chopped garlic

1 tbsp finely chopped fresh galangal or root ginger

4 kaffir lime leaves or 2 tsp shredded lime zest

1 tbsp fish sauce (nam pla)

2 tsp sugar

1 x 400 ml (14fl oz) tin of coconut milk

a handful of fresh coriander leaves

50g (2oz) roasted peanuts, chopped

1 large, fresh red chilli, de-seeded and shredded

salt

Step one Cut the chicken into 2.5cm (1in) chunks. Peel off the tough outer layers of the sticks of lemon grass, leaving the tender whitish centre, and chop it finely.

Step two Heat a wok or large frying pan until it is very hot and add the oil. Add the red curry paste and stir-fry for 2 minutes, then add the chicken and potatoes and mix until they are coated with the paste.

Step three Add the lemon grass, shallots, garlic, galangal or ginger, lime leaves or zest, fish sauce, sugar and 1 teaspoon of salt and stir-fry for another minute.

Step four Pour in the coconut milk and 3 tablespoons of water, turn the heat to low and simmer for 15 minutes or until the chicken is cooked through. Add the coriander, stir and garnish with the chopped peanuts and chilli. Serve at once.

Stir-fried Thai Green Curry Chicken with Aubergines

This dish takes a little longer to prepare, but I couldn't resist including it here – Thai cooking is full of many fragrant and enticing aromas, and this is no exception. Thai curry pastes are time-consuming and laborious to make but, fortunately, there are now high-quality Thai pastes available at the supermarket.

Step one If using chicken thighs on the bone, remove the skin and bones from the chicken thighs or have your butcher do it for you.

Step two Preheat the oven to 200°C/400°F/gas 6. If you are using Chinese aubergines, roast them for 20 minutes; if you are using large aubergines, roast them for about 30–40 minutes or until they are soft and cooked through. Allow the aubergines to cool and then peel them. Put them in a colander and let them drain for 30 minutes or more. Chop the aubergine flesh. This procedure can be done hours in advance.

Step three Cut the chicken into 2.5cm (1in) chunks and combine them in a bowl with the soy sauce, rice wine or sherry, sesame oil and cornflour. Heat a wok or large frying pan until it is very hot; then add the oil, then the chicken. Stir-fry for 5 minutes, then remove the chicken and drain off most of the fat and oil, leaving 2 teaspoons. Return the drained chicken to the wok or pan and add the garlic, ginger and spring onions and stir-fry for 5 minutes. Then add the chopped aubergine flesh and all the remaining ingredients except the basil leaves. Continue to cook for another 3 minutes, stirring from time to time. When the chicken is cooked, add the basil leaves and give the mixture a good stir. Transfer to a platter and serve at once.

Serves 4

450g (1lb) boneless skinless chicken thighs or 900g (2lb) chicken thighs on the bone

1kg (2lb 4oz) Chinese or ordinary aubergines

2 tsp light soy sauce

2 tsp Shaoxing rice wine or dry sherry

1 tsp sesame oil

2 tsp cornflour

1½ tbsp ground nut oil

3 tbsp chopped garlic

1 tbsp finely chopped fresh root ginger

3 tbsp finely chopped spring onions

2–3 tbsp Thai green curry paste

1 tbsp fish sauce (nam pla) or light soy sauce

2 tsp sugar

a large handful of fresh basil leaves

Stir-fried Chicken with Chinese and Button Mushrooms

A chicken stir fry is such an easy and appetising dish to serve.

Serves 4

450g (1lb) boneless
skinless chicken
thighs or 900g (2lb)
chicken thighs on the
bone

for the marinade

2 tsp light soy sauce

2 tsp Shaoxing rice
wine or dry sherry

1 tsp sesame oil

2 tsp cornflour

for the stir fry

25g (1oz) dried
Chinese mushrooms

350g (12oz) button
mushrooms

1½ tbsp ground nut oil

1 onion, thinly sliced

2 tbsp coarsely
chopped garlic

2 tsp finely chopped
orange zest

2 tbsp Shaoxing rice
wine or dry sherry

3 tbsp oyster sauce

2 tsp sugar

a large handful of fresh
basil leaves

salt and pepper

Step one Remove the skin and bones from the unboned chicken thighs, if using, or have the butcher do it for you. Cut the chicken into 2.5cm (1in) chunks and combine them in a bowl with the soy sauce, rice wine or sherry, sesame oil and cornflour. Allow to marinate for 20 minutes at room temperature.

Step two Meanwhile, soak the Chinese mushrooms in warm water for 20 minutes. Drain them, squeeze out the excess liquid and discard all the water. Remove and discard the stems and cut the caps into thick strips. Slice the button mushrooms. Heat a wok or large frying pan until it is very hot, add the oil and then the chicken. Stir-fry for 5 minutes, until the chicken is brown. Remove the chicken and drain off most of the oil, leaving just 2 teaspoons. Reheat the wok or pan until it is hot, quickly add the onion and garlic and stir-fry for 2 minutes. Then add the Chinese mushrooms, button mushrooms, 2 teaspoons of salt and ½ teaspoon of pepper and stir-fry for 1 minute.

Step three Now, return the chicken to the wok or pan and add the orange zest and remaining rice wine or sherry and continue to stir-fry for 4 minutes, or until the liquid has been absorbed by the mushrooms or has evaporated. Finally, add the oyster sauce, sugar and basil leaves, give the mixture a good stir and cook for another minute. Serve at once.

Classic Vietnamese Lemon Grass Chicken

In this hearty dish, lemon grass lends a fragrant flavour to chicken. It does take a little time, but is quite easy to make and will satisfy a large, hungry family. You could ask your butcher to joint the chicken for you. Serve with noodles or plain rice.

Step one Blot the chicken dry with kitchen paper. Peel off the tough outer layers of the sticks of lemon grass, leaving the tender, whitish centre. Crush with the flat of a knife, then cut into 7.5cm (3in) pieces.

Step two In a large bowl, combine all the ingredients for the marinade, season with 1 teaspoon of salt and ½ teaspoon of pepper and add the chicken. Leave the mixture to marinate at room temperature for 45 minutes. Heat a wok or large frying pan over a high heat. Add the oil and, when it is very hot and slightly smoking, add the chicken, together with the marinade, and stir-fry for 5 minutes. Then add the onions, garlic and chillies and continue to stir-fry for 10 minutes.

Step three Add the sugar and peanuts and stir-fry for 2 minutes. Finally, add the fish sauce or light soy sauce and stir-fry for just 2 minutes, mixing all the ingredients well. Transfer the mixture to a platter and serve at once.

Serves 4–6

1 small chicken, weighing about 900g–1kg (2–2¼ lb), jointed into small pieces

2 tbsp ground nut oil

175g (6oz) onions, finely sliced

6 garlic cloves, crushed

2 fresh red or green chillies, de-seeded and coarsely chopped

2 tsp sugar

100g (4oz) roasted peanuts, coarsely chopped

3 tbsp fish sauce (nam pla) or light soy sauce

for the marinade

5 sticks of lemon grass

3 tbsp finely chopped spring onions

salt and pepper

For more recipes from My Kitchen Table, sign up for our newsletter at www.mykitchentable.co.uk/newsletter

Wolfgang Puck's Stir-fried Chicken with Garlic and Fresh Coriander

One of the best practitioners of Fusion cooking is Wolfgang Puck, who made his reputation as a chef to Hollywood stars.

Serves 4–6

450g (1lb) boneless skinless chicken thighs

1 tbsp Shaoxing rice wine or dry sherry

1 tbsp light soy sauce

2 tsp sesame oil

2 tsp cornflour

pepper

for the vinaigrette

3 tbsp white rice vinegar

2 tbsp light soy sauce

2 tbsp ground nut oil

1 tbsp sesame oil

1 tbsp lemon juice

salt and pepper

for the stir fry

225g (8oz) red or green peppers

2½ tbsp ground nut oil

3 tbsp garlic

6 tbsp spring onions

3 tbsp Shaoxing rice wine or dry sherry

2 tsp sesame oil

3 tbsp coriander

225g (8oz) iceberg lettuce

Step one Cut the chicken into 2.5cm (1in) chunks and combine them in a bowl with the rice wine or sherry, soy sauce, sesame oil, cornflour and 1 teaspoon of pepper. Leave to marinate for 20 minutes.

Step two Make the vinaigrette by combining the vinegar, soy sauce, ground nut and sesame oils, lemon juice, ½ teaspoon of salt and ¼ teaspoon of pepper in a small bowl. Mix well and set aside. Meanwhile, de-seed the peppers and cut into small dice.

Step three Heat a wok or large frying pan over a high heat until it is hot. Add 1½ tablespoons of the oil and, when it is very hot and slightly smoking, stir-fry the chicken for about 5 minutes. Remove the chicken, drain in a colander and put into a bowl. Wipe the wok or pan clean. Reheat the wok or pan over a high heat and, when it is hot, add the remaining tablespoon of ground nut oil. When it is smoking slightly, thinly slice and add the garlic and stir-fry for 30 seconds. Then finely slice and add both the peppers and spring onions and stir-fry for another minute. Now add the rice wine or sherry and sesame oil and stir-fry for 1 minute; return the chicken to the mixture and continue to stir-fry for 1 minute, mixing well. Finely chop and add the coriander and mix well.

Step four Turn onto a platter. Gently separate the lettuce leaves and arrange around the platter. Pour the vinaigrette into a small bowl and serve at once. Each diner puts some chicken mixture on lettuce leaves, adds the vinaigrette and then eats with his or her hands.

Delectable Broccoli Chicken

Chicken and broccoli are a wonderful combination. In this Vietnamese-inspired recipe, the chicken is first marinated, then fried and then it is paired with crunchy green broccoli.

Step one Separate the broccoli heads into small florets and peel and slice the stems. Bring a large pan of salted water to the boil and put the broccoli pieces in to blanch for several minutes, then immerse them in cold water. Drain thoroughly.

Step two Cut the chicken into 2.5cm (1in) pieces and, to marinate, combine them with the pepper, fish sauce and light soy sauce. Mix well and allow to marinate for 30 minutes. Dust the chicken pieces with cornflour, shaking off any excess.

Step three Heat a wok or large frying pan over a high heat until it is hot. Add the 400ml (14fl oz) of oil and, when it is very hot and slightly smoking, deep-fry the chicken pieces for 8 minutes or until they are golden brown. Remove them with a slotted spoon and drain on kitchen paper. You may have to do this in two or more batches.

Step four Drain off all the oil. Reheat the wok and add the 1 tbsp of oil. When it is hot, add the garlic and onion and stir-fry for 1 minute. Then add the blanched broccoli and continue to stir-fry for 1 minute. Add the rice wine or sherry and stock or water and continue to stir-fry at a moderate to high heat for 4 minutes until the broccoli is thoroughly heated through. Add the tomatoes, oyster sauce, fish sauce, sugar, sesame oil, 1 teaspoon of salt and ½ teaspoon of pepper and continue to stir-fry for 30 seconds, then add the drained chicken and stir-fry for 2 minutes or until the chicken is thoroughly heated through. Transfer to a warm platter and serve at once.

Serves 4

450g (1lb) fresh broccoli

450g (1lb) boneless skinless chicken thighs

400ml (14fl oz) plus 1 tbsp ground nut oil

3 tbsp coarsely chopped garlic

1 small onion, quartered

2 tbsp Shaoxing rice wine or dry sherry

3 tbsp home-made or good-quality bought chicken stock or water

225g (8oz) tomatoes, quartered

3 tbsp oyster sauce

2 tbsp fish sauce (nam pla)

1 tsp sugar

2 tsp sesame oil

salt and pepper

for the marinade

½ tsp freshly ground pepper

1 tbsp fish sauce (nam pla)

1 tsp light soy sauce

cornflour, for dusting

Thai-style Chicken

I greatly enjoy the Thai way with chicken. The combination of exotic lemon grass, garlic and fresh chillies always has my mouth watering. The Thais have their own type of wok and stir-fry many of their dishes. In this Thai-inspired dish, I have used some Thai flavourings and created my own tasty chicken dish. It works brilliantly with rice.

Serves 4

450g (1lb) boneless skinless chicken thighs or 900g (2lb) chicken thighs with bone in

1 stick of lemon grass

1 tbsp ground nut oil

1 onion, thinly sliced

2 tbsp coarsely chopped garlic

2 tsp finely chopped lime zest

3 fresh red or green chillies, de-seeded and finely shredded

2 tsp sugar

a large handful of fresh basil leaves

salt

for the marinade

2 tsp light soy sauce

2 tsp Shaoxing rice wine or dry sherry

1 tsp sesame oil

2 tsp cornflour

Step one If you are using unboned thighs, remove the skin and bones from the chicken thighs or have your butcher do it for you. Cut the chicken into 2.5cm (1in) chunks and, to marinate, combine it in a bowl with the soy sauce, rice wine or sherry, sesame oil and cornflour. Leave to marinate for 20 minutes.

Step two Peel the stick of lemon grass to reveal the tender, whitish centre and cut into 5cm (2in) pieces. Smash them with the flat of a knife or cleaver.

Step three Heat a wok or large frying pan until it is very hot. Add the oil, then the chicken and stir-fry for 5 minutes until the chicken is brown. Remove the chicken and drain off the oil. Return the drained chicken to the wok and add the remainder of the ingredients, except the basil leaves, and season with 2 teaspoons of salt. Continue to cook for another 8–10 minutes, stirring from time to time, until the chicken is cooked. Add the basil leaves and give the mixture a good stir. Pour onto a warm platter and serve at once.

For Ken Hom's guide to ingredients, go to
www.mykitchentable.co.uk/authors/KenHom/ingredients

Thai-style Duck

I often think that duck is a neglected food. Fortuitously, duck breasts are now available in many supermarkets. They are perfect for a quick stir fry and can add a new dimension to your cooking repertoire.

Step one Cut the duck breasts into slices 4cm (1½in) long and 1cm (½in) thick. Put the duck slices in a bowl, add all the marinade ingredients along with ½ teaspoon of salt and some pepper and mix well. Let the slices steep in the marinade for about 15 minutes.

Step two Peel the stick of lemon grass to reveal the tender, whitish centre and cut it into 5cm (2in) pieces. Crush with the flat of a cleaver or knife and set aside. Heat a wok or large frying pan over a high heat until it is very hot. Add the oil and, when it is very hot and slightly smoking, add the duck from the marinade and stir-fry for about 2 minutes; it should be slightly pink in the centre. Remove the duck and drain it in a colander.

Step three Pour off all but 1½ tablespoons of the oil from the pan and reheat it over a high heat. Add the lemon grass, shallots and garlic and stir-fry for 3 minutes. Now add the fish sauce or light soy sauce, dark soy sauce, lime zest, chilli peppers and sugar and stir-fry for 1 minute.

Step four Return the drained duck to the wok or pan. Stir to mix well, toss in the basil leaves, give it a good stir and transfer to a platter. Serve at once.

Serves 4

450g (1lb) boneless skinless duck breasts

1 stick of lemon grass

3 tbsp ground nut oil

3 tbsp finely sliced shallots

2 tbsp coarsely chopped garlic

1 tbsp fish sauce (nam pla) or light soy sauce

1 tsp dark soy sauce

2 tsp finely grated lime zest

3 large, fresh red or green chilli peppers, de-seeded and finely shredded

2 tsp sugar

a large handful of fresh basil leaves

for the marinade

2 tsp light soy sauce

2 tsp Shaoxing rice wine or dry sherry

2 tsp sesame oil

2 tsp cornflour

salt and pepper

For a video masterclass on marinating meat, go to
www.mykitchentable.co.uk/videos/marinatingmeat

Spicy Pork with Fragrant Basil

This is a mouth-watering Thai-inspired dish. The minced pork is quickly stir-fried and tossed with so much fragrant basil that the herb almost plays the role of a green vegetable. Thai cookery, it seems, can never use too much basil. And here it is used to such good effect, helping to produce a marvellously aromatic dish that goes extremely well with plain rice. It is ideal for a quick but exotic family meal.

Serves 2–4

1½ tbsp ground nut oil

3 tbsp coarsely chopped garlic

3 tbsp de-seeded and finely chopped red chilli peppers

450g (1lb) minced pork

2 tbsp finely chopped fresh coriander

2 tbsp fish sauce (nam pla)

1 tbsp oyster sauce

2 tsp sugar

150ml (¼ pint) home-made or good-quality bought chicken stock

a large handful of fresh basil leaves

Step one Heat a wok or large frying pan over a high heat and add the oil. When it is very hot and slightly smoking, add the garlic and chilli peppers and stir-fry for 30 seconds.

Step two Add the pork and stir-fry for 3 minutes. Then add the coriander, fish sauce, oyster sauce, sugar and stock and continue to stir-fry for 3 minutes.

Step three Add the basil and stir-fry for another minute. Turn onto a warm platter and serve at once.

Stir-fried Chilli Pork with Cashews

Pork, the preferred Chinese 'red meat', is delicious when combined
with the taste and texture of nuts – in this case, cashews. A touch of chilli
bean sauce is added for zest and you have a quick, savoury dish good
enough to grace the centre of any family table. Serve with plain rice and
a vegetable dish for a satisfying meal.

Step one Cut the pork into thin slices 5cm (2in) long. Put it in a
bowl and mix in all the marinade ingredients. Leave for around
10–15 minutes, so that the pork has time to absorb the flavours
of the marinade.

Step two Heat a wok or frying pan over a very high heat and
add the oil. When it is very hot and slightly smoking, add the
pork slices, 1 teaspoon of salt and ⅓ teaspoon of pepper and
stir-fry for 2 minutes. Remove the pork with a slotted spoon.

Step three Add the cashew nuts and stir-fry for 1 minute, then
add all the remainder of the ingredients except the spring
onions. Return the pork to the wok or pan and stir-fry for around
2 minutes. Garnish with the spring onions and serve at once.

Serves 4

450g (1lb) lean
boneless pork chops

1½ tbsp ground nut oil

4 tbsp cashew nuts

1 tbsp Shaoxing rice
wine or dry sherry

1 tbsp light soy sauce

1 tbsp chilli bean
sauce

2 tsp sugar

1 tbsp finely chopped
spring onions

salt and pepper

for the marinade

1 tbsp Shaoxing rice
wine or dry sherry

2 tsp light soy sauce

2 tsp sesame oil

1 tsp cornflour

Stir-fried Pork with Mushrooms

This is a tasty dish that can easily be served with noodles or pasta. It combines savoury pork with mushrooms in an earthy, spicy mixture. Once made, it can easily be reheated.

Serves 4

1 tbsp ground nut oil

3 tbsp coarsely chopped garlic

2 tbsp de-seeded and finely chopped red chilli peppers

225g (8oz) minced pork

2 tbsp finely chopped spring onions

2 tbsp light soy sauce

2 tsp sugar

a large handful of fresh basil leaves

2 tsp sesame oil

for the mushrooms

1 tbsp ground nut oil

225g (8oz) button mushrooms, sliced

1 tbsp Shaoxing rice wine or dry sherry

salt and pepper

Step one Heat a wok or large frying pan over a high heat and add the ground nut oil. When it is very hot and slightly smoking, put in the garlic and chilli peppers and stir-fry for 30 seconds. Then add the pork and stir-fry for 3 minutes. Add the spring onions, soy sauce, sugar and 3 tablespoons of water. Stir-fry for 3 minutes then add the basil and stir-fry for another minute. Remove the mixture from the wok and set aside.

Step two To cook the mushrooms, wipe the wok clean and reheat it over a high heat. Add the ground nut oil and, when it is very hot and slightly smoking, add the mushrooms and stir-fry them for about a minute.

Step three Add the rice wine or sherry and a little salt and pepper and stir-fry for about 5 minutes, until the mushrooms are cooked through and have re-absorbed any remaining liquid.

Step four Return the pork mixture to the wok, combine with the mushrooms and stir-fry for 2 minutes or until heated through. Just before serving, add the sesame oil and give the mixture a couple of quick stirs. Turn it onto a warm serving dish and serve at once.

Stir-fried Pork with Spring Onions

This recipe illustrates the relative ease of using a wok. A basic stir-fried meat dish can be made in minutes. The key to success is not to overcook the pork.

Step one Cut the pork into thin slices, 5cm (2in) long.

Step two Put the sliced pork into a bowl and mix in all the marinade ingredients. Leave for 10–15 minutes so that the pork absorbs the flavours of the marinade.

Step three Heat a wok to a very high heat, then add the ground nut oil. When it is very hot and slightly smoking, add the pork slices and stir-fry for about 2 minutes, until brown. Remove the meat with a slotted spoon and leave to drain in a colander.

Step four Reheat the wok and add the spring onions, sugar, 1 teaspoon of salt and ½ teaspoon of pepper. Stir-fry for 2 minutes or until the spring onions are wilted. Return the pork to the wok and stir-fry for another 2 minutes or until heated through. Serve at once.

Serves 3–4

450g (1lb) lean boneless pork

1 tbsp ground nut oil

8 spring onions, cut on the diagonal into 5cm (2in) lengths

1 tsp sugar

salt and pepper

for the marinade

1 tbsp Shaoxing rice wine or dry sherry

1 tbsp light soy sauce

2 tsp sesame oil

1 tsp cornflour

Singapore Pork Satay

I love eating in Singapore and this pork satay is a personal favourite.

Serves 4

450g (1lb) thick
boneless pork chops

for the peanut sauce

2 tbsp garlic

3 tbsp shallots

1 tbsp fresh root
ginger

2 red chillies

1 tbsp ground nut oil

1 tbsp lemon juice

2 tbsp coconut milk

1 tbsp light soy sauce

1 tsp dark soy sauce

1 tsp sugar

175g (6oz) roasted
peanuts, coarsely
chopped

salt and pepper

for the marinade

2 tbsp light soy sauce

1 tbsp Shaoxing rice
wine or dry sherry

2 tbsp finely chopped
garlic

1 tsp freshly ground
pepper

2 tsp sesame oil

1 tsp sugar

2 tsp five-spice
powder

salt

Step one Cut the pork into thin slices, about 2.5cm (1in) wide and 7.5cm (3in) long. In a large bowl, combine the pork slices with all the marinade ingredients. Leave to marinate overnight in the fridge.

Step two Meanwhile, make the peanut sauce. Coarsely chop the garlic and shallots, and finely chop the ginger. De-seed and chop the red chillies. Heat a wok or frying pan, add the ground nut oil and, when it is slightly smoking, add the garlic, shallots, ginger and chillies and stir-fry for 1 minute. Then add the lemon juice, coconut milk, light and dark soy sauce, sugar, some salt and pepper and 250ml (8fl oz) of water. Cook for 5 minutes, then add the peanuts and mix well.

Step three Continue to simmer the sauce until you get the consistency you like. Add more water if you prefer it slightly thinner. Remove from the heat and leave to cool. Meanwhile, soak some bamboo skewers in cold water for 15 minutes. Thread the pork onto the skewers and set aside.

Step four Prepare a barbecue or preheat a ridged grill pan or the oven grill. When the charcoal is ash white or the grill is very hot, cook the satay for 2 minutes on each side, until golden brown. Serve at once with the peanut sauce.

Pork with Shrimp Paste

In this dish, called *moo phad gapi*, tender pork fillet is marinated in dark soy sauce and flavoured with aromatic shrimp paste to make a special Thai treat. Serve with your favourite stir-fried vegetable dish and plain steamed rice for a satisfying meal.

Step one Cut the pork into thin slices about 4cm (1½in) long and place in a bowl. Add 1 teaspoon of salt and the dark soy sauce, mix well and leave to marinate for 20 minutes.

Step two Heat a wok or large frying pan over a high heat until it is very hot, then add the oil. When it is very hot and slightly smoking, add the marinated pork and stir-fry for about 2 minutes. Remove with a slotted spoon and drain in a colander.

Step three Quickly add the chillies, onion and shallots to the wok and stir-fry for 2 minutes. Then add the fish sauce, light soy sauce, sugar, shrimp paste and ½ teaspoon of white pepper. Return the drained pork to the wok and stir-fry for 2 minutes or until the pork is cooked through. Add the coriander leaves, give the mixture a good stir and serve at once.

Serves 4

450g (1lb) pork fillet

salt

1 tbsp dark soy sauce

1½ tbsp vegetable oil

2 small, fresh red or green Thai chillies, de-seeded and chopped

1 small onion, coarsely chopped

2 tbsp finely sliced shallots

2 tbsp fish sauce (nam pla)

1 tbsp light soy sauce

1 tsp sugar

1½ tsp shrimp paste

white pepper

a handful of fresh coriander leaves

KITCHEN TABLE

Have you made this recipe? Tell us what you think at www.mykitchentable.co.uk/blog

Stir-fried Minced Pork with Basil

This simple family dish, called *moo phad bai horapa*, is quick and easy to make. The basil is the key to its success; its fresh green colour, distinctive aroma and unique flavour work to make something very Thai and very special. Serve with rice or noodles and a vegetable.

Serves 2–4

1½ tbsp vegetable oil

1 tbsp Thai red curry paste

3 tbsp coarsely chopped garlic

3 tbsp finely sliced shallots

450g (1lb) minced pork

2 tbsp fish sauce (nam pla)

3 tbsp coconut milk

2 tsp sugar

a very large handful of fresh Thai basil leaves or ordinary basil leaves, chopped

Step one Heat a wok or large frying pan over a medium heat and add the oil. When it is very hot and slightly smoking, add the curry paste and stir-fry gently for 1 minute, until it begins to melt.

Step two Add the garlic and shallots and stir-fry for a minute longer. Then add the pork and stir-fry for 3 minutes.

Step three Now add the fish sauce, coconut milk and sugar and stir-fry for 3 minutes longer. Finally, add the chopped basil to the wok or pan and stir-fry for another minute. Serve at once.

Stir-fried Garlic Pork

Garlic and pork are two very familiar ingredients in Chinese cuisine. My mother often made this dish and it has always been a favourite of mine. She would vary the taste once in a while by adding a dash of spicy chilli bean sauce. An easy dish to make in the wok, it goes perfectly with plain rice and any stir-fried vegetable.

Step one Cut the pork into thin slices 5cm (2in) long. Put the slices in a small bowl and mix them well with the rice wine or sherry, soy sauce, sesame oil and cornflour. Leave to marinate for about 20 minutes.

Step two Heat a wok or large frying pan until it is hot. Add half the oil and, when it is very hot and almost smoking, lift the pork out of the marinade with a slotted spoon, put it in the wok and quickly stir-fry for about 2–3 minutes. Drain well. Wipe the wok clean, reheat it and add the remainder of the oil then quickly add the garlic, spring onions and chilli bean sauce.

Step three A few seconds later add the remainder of the ingredients. Bring the mixture to a boil and then return the pork to the wok or pan. Stir-fry the entire mixture for another 5 minutes. Turn it onto a warm platter and serve at once.

Serves 4

450g (1lb) lean pork

2 tbsp ground nut oil

3 tbsp finely chopped garlic

3 spring onions, thinly sliced diagonally

2 tsp chilli bean sauce

3 tbsp black beans

1 tbsp light soy sauce

1 tsp Shaoxing rice wine or dry sherry

1 tsp sugar

1 tbsp home-made or good-quality bought chicken stock or water

1 tbsp sesame oil

for the marinade

1 tbsp Shaoxing rice wine or dry sherry

1 tbsp light soy sauce

2 tsp sesame oil

1 tsp cornflour

Beef with Peppercorns

The Chinese often find large pieces of beef intimidating, preferring to cut meat into slices and stir-fry it quickly, as in this recipe. The result is a fast dish that combines fusion elements of East and West to give a unique slant on a classic. Serve with noodles.

Serves 4

450g (1lb) lean beef steak

3 tbsp ground nut oil

2 tbsp cognac

100g (4oz) shallots, finely chopped

2 tbsp black peppercorns, lightly crushed

250ml (8fl oz) home-made or good-quality bought chicken stock

25g (1oz) butter, cut into small pieces

salt

for the marinade

1 tbsp light soy sauce

1 tbsp Shaoxing rice wine or dry sherry

2 tsp cornflour

2 tsp sesame oil

Step one Cut the beef into slices 5cm (2in) long and 5mm (¼in) thick, cutting against the grain. Put the beef in a bowl with all the marinade ingredients, mix well, and leave to marinate for about 20 minutes.

Step two Heat a wok or large frying pan over a high heat until it is very hot. Add the oil and, when it is very hot and slightly smoking, remove the beef from the marinade with a slotted spoon. Add it to the pan and stir-fry for 2 minutes, until it is barely cooked. Remove and leave to drain in a colander or sieve set inside a bowl.

Step three Pour out all the oil, reheat the wok or pan over a high heat, then add the cognac. Deglaze by stirring and scraping the base of the pan with a wooden spoon. Quickly add the shallots, peppercorns, ½ teaspoon of salt and the stock and simmer over a high heat until reduced by half. Stir in the butter, piece by piece.

Step four Return the beef to the wok or pan and stir-fry for 30 seconds to warm it through. Serve at once.

Fragrant Beef with Peppers

Here, I have adapted the Thai version of this dish by pairing the lemon grass with sweet red or green peppers, which add colour as well as contrasting taste and texture.

Step one Cut the beef into thin slices 5cm (2in) long, cutting against the grain. Put it into a bowl together with all the marinade ingredients, mix well, and leave to marinate for about 20 minutes.

Step two Peel the sticks of lemon grass to reveal the tender, whitish centre. Crush with the flat of a knife and cut into 5cm (2in) pieces, then set aside.

Step three Heat a wok or large frying pan over a high heat until it is very hot. Add the ground nut oil and, when it is very hot and slightly smoking, remove the beef from the marinade with a slotted spoon. Add it to the pan and stir-fry for 3–5 minutes, until browned. Remove and leave to drain in a colander or sieve set inside a bowl.

Step four Pour off all but 1 tablespoon of the oil from the wok or pan. Reheat over a high heat and then add the sticks of lemon grass, ginger, shallots and garlic and stir-fry for 20 seconds.

Step five Add the peppers, soy sauce, rice wine or dry sherry, sugar and ½ teaspoon each of salt and pepper and continue to stir-fry for 3 minutes. Then return the beef to the wok and stir-fry for 4 minutes, mixing well. Drizzle in the sesame oil and give the mixture a few stirs. Transfer to a warm platter and serve straight away.

Serves 4

450g (1lb) lean beef steak

3 sticks of lemon grass

3 tbsp ground nut oil

2 tsp finely chopped fresh root ginger

100g (4oz) shallots, thinly sliced

3 garlic cloves, thinly sliced

225g (8oz) red or green peppers (about 1 large or 2 small), de-seeded and cut into 2.5cm (1in) pieces

1 tbsp light soy sauce

1½ tbsp Shaoxing rice wine or dry sherry

1½ tsp sugar

3 tsp sesame oil

salt and pepper

for the marinade

1 tbsp light soy sauce

1 tbsp Shaoxing rice wine or dry sherry

2 tsp sesame oil

2 tsp cornflour

Vietnamese-style Lemon Grass Beef

Beef goes especially well with lemon grass in this Vietnamese-inspired recipe, which is a personal favourite of mine.

Serves 4

450g (1lb) lean beef steak

3 tbsp ground nut oil

100g (4oz) onions, thinly sliced

2 fresh red or green chilli peppers, de-seeded and coarsely chopped

3 tbsp coarsely chopped garlic

1 tbsp Shaoxing rice wine or dry sherry

2 tsp sugar

for the marinade

2 sticks of lemon grass

2 tsp fish sauce (nam pla)

2 tsp Shaoxing rice wine or dry sherry

2 tsp sesame oil

2 tsp cornflour

salt and pepper

to garnish

25g (1oz) roasted peanuts, coarsely chopped

a handful of fresh coriander sprigs

Step one Put the beef in the freezer for 20 minutes. This will allow it to harden slightly for easier cutting. Meanwhile, peel the sticks of lemon grass to reveal the tender, whitish centre. Crush with the flat of a knife and cut into pieces 7.5cm (3in) long. Cut the beef into very thin slices, 4cm (1½in) long. Put them in a bowl with all the marinade ingredients, including the lemon grass. Season with ½ teaspoon of salt and ¼ teaspoon of pepper, mix well and leave to marinate for 30 minutes.

Step two Heat a wok or large frying pan over a high heat until it is very hot. Add the ground nut oil and, when it is very hot and slightly smoking, add the beef, plus the marinade, and stir-fry for about 2 minutes. Remove the meat and drain in a colander or sieve set inside a bowl.

Step three Pour off all but 1½ tablespoons of the oil and reheat the wok or pan over a high heat. Add the onions, chilli peppers and garlic and stir-fry for 1 minute. Then add the rice wine or dry sherry and sugar and stir-fry for 3 minutes.

Step four Quickly return the meat to the wok and continue to stir-fry for 2 minutes or until the beef is heated through. Turn the mixture onto a warm platter, garnish with the chopped peanuts and coriander and serve at once.

Stir-fried Beef with Oyster Sauce

This used to be one of the most popular dishes in my family's restaurant, especially with Westerners. It is very savoury and quite addictive. Buy the best brand of oyster sauce you can find. Good oyster sauce does not taste at all fishy, rather, it has a meaty flavour and goes very well with beef or pork. This simple dish is delicious served with plain steamed rice.

Step one Cut the beef into slices 5cm (2in) long and 5mm (¼in) thick, cutting against the grain of the meat. Put them in a bowl. Mix in the soy sauce, sesame oil, rice wine or sherry and cornflour. Leave to marinate for 20 minutes.

Step two Heat a wok until it is very hot, then add the ground nut oil. When it is very hot and slightly smoking, add the beef slices and stir-fry for 5 minutes or until lightly browned.

Step three Remove the meat from the wok and drain well in a colander set inside a bowl. Discard the drained oil.

Step four Wipe the wok clean and reheat it over a high heat. Add the oyster sauce and bring it to a simmer.

Step five Return the drained beef slices to the wok and toss them thoroughly with the oyster sauce. Turn the mixture onto a serving platter, garnish with the spring onions and serve straight away.

Serves 4

450g (1lb) lean beef steak

1 tbsp light soy sauce

2 tsp sesame oil

1 tbsp Shaoxing rice wine or dry sherry

2 tsp cornflour

3 tbsp ground nut oil

3 tbsp oyster sauce

1½ tbsp finely chopped spring onions, to garnish

For more recipes from My Kitchen Table, sign up for our newsletter at www.mykitchentable.co.uk/newsletter

KITCHEN
TABLE

Malaysian-style Beef Satay

This satay is easy to prepare and makes a lovely starter or main.

Serves 4

450g (1lb) beef fillet

for the marinade

3 tbsp shallots

2 tbsp garlic

1 tbsp light soy sauce

1 tbsp vegetable oil

2 tsp ground turmeric

2 tsp ground cumin

2 tsp ground fennel seeds

1 tsp ground coriander

2 tsp sugar

2 tsp finely grated lemon zest

salt and pepper

for the peanut sauce

2 tbsp garlic

3 tbsp shallots

1 tbsp fresh root ginger

2 red chillies

175g (6oz) roasted peanuts

1 tbsp ground nut oil

1 tbsp lemon juice

2 tbsp coconut milk

1 tbsp light soy sauce

1 tsp dark soy sauce

1 tsp sugar

salt and pepper

Step one Cut the beef fillet into 2.5cm (1in) cubes and finely chop the shallots and garlic for the marinade. In a large bowl, combine the beef with all the marinade ingredients and season with a little salt and 1 teaspoon of pepper. Leave to marinate for 1 hour at room temperature.

Step two Meanwhile, make the peanut sauce. Coarsely chop the garlic and shallots, and finely chop the ginger. De-seed and chop the red chillies, then coarsely grind the peanuts in a food-processor. Heat a wok or frying pan, add the ground nut oil and, when it is slightly smoking, add the garlic, shallots, ginger and chillies and stir-fry for 1 minute. Then add the lemon juice, coconut milk, light and dark soy sauce and sugar. Pour in 250ml (8fl oz) of water and add some salt and pepper. Cook for 5 minutes, then add the coarsely ground peanuts and mix well.

Step three Continue to simmer the sauce until you get the consistency you like. Add more water if you prefer it slightly thinner. Remove from the heat and leave to cool (the sauce should be served at room temperature).

Step four Soak some bamboo skewers in a little cold water for 15 minutes. Thread the beef onto the skewers and set aside.

Step five Prepare a barbecue or preheat a ridged chargrill pan or the oven grill. When the charcoal is ash white or the grill is very hot, cook the satay for 2 minutes on each side, or until done to your liking. Serve at once with the peanut sauce.

Mussaman-style Beef Curry

This delicious curry dish takes time to prepare, but it is one of my favourite recipes. I promise the end result is well worth the wait!

Step one Cut the beef into 5cm (2in) cubes. Heat a wok or large frying pan and add the oil. When it is very hot and slightly smoking, add the beef and fry for about 10 minutes, until it is brown all over (you will need to do this in several batches to get the best results).

Step two Pour off any excess fat, leaving 1 tablespoon of oil in the pan. Put all the meat back in the pan, add the Mussaman curry paste and stir-fry with the beef for about 5 minutes. Transfer this mixture to a large casserole or pot.

Step three For the sauce, peel off the tough outer layers of the sticks of lemon grass, leaving the tender whitish centre. Cut it into 7.5cm (3in) pieces, crush with the flat of a heavy knife, then add to the casserole with all the remainder of the braising sauce ingredients. Bring to the boil, skim off any fat from the surface and turn the heat down as low as possible. Cover and braise for 1 hour.

Step four Peel and add the potatoes to the casserole and cook for another 30 minutes or until the meat is quite tender. Then remove the lid, turn the heat up to high and boil rapidly for about 15 minutes to reduce and thicken the sauce. Garnish with the chopped peanuts and coriander before serving.

Serves 4–6

1.5kg (3lb) stewing beef, such as brisket or shin

2 tbsp vegetable oil

3 tbsp Mussaman curry paste

225g (8oz) small new potatoes

3 tbsp chopped roasted peanuts

a handful of fresh coriander leaves

for the braising sauce

2 sticks of lemon grass

1.2 litres (2 pints) tinned coconut milk

600ml (1 pint) hot water

3 tbsp sugar

3 tbsp fish sauce (nam pla)

2 tbsp lime juice

2 tsp shrimp paste

3 tbsp finely sliced shallots

2 cinnamon sticks

6 cardamom pods

¼ tsp freshly grated nutmeg

4 kaffir lime leaves or 1 tbsp shredded lime zest

For step-by-step photographs of this recipe, go to www.mykitchentable.co.uk/recipes/mussaman

Savoury Beef with Asparagus

Asparagus is the favourite vegetable of many lovers of good food. It is easy to see why. The cooked stalks combine crunchy and soft textures, subtle and distinct flavours.

Serves 4

450g (1lb) lean beef steak

450g (1lb) fresh asparagus

3 tbsp ground nut oil

100g (4oz) onions, thinly sliced

2 tbsp black beans, coarsely chopped

1½ tbsp finely chopped garlic

2 tsp finely chopped fresh root ginger

3 tbsp home-made or good-quality bought chicken stock or water

1 tbsp Shaoxing rice wine or dry sherry

1 tsp sugar

salt and pepper

2 tbsp oyster sauce

for the marinade

2 tsp light soy sauce

2 tsp Shaoxing rice wine or dry sherry

2 tsp sesame oil

2 tsp cornflour

salt and pepper

Step one Put the beef in the freezer for 20 minutes. This will allow the meat to harden slightly for easier cutting. Cut it into thin slices, each 4cm (1½in) long. Put the beef slices in a bowl and add the soy sauce, rice wine or sherry, sesame oil, cornflour, ½ teaspoon of salt and ¼ teaspoon of pepper. Mix well and let the slices steep in the marinade for 15 minutes. Meanwhile, slice the asparagus on the diagonal into 7.5cm (3in) pieces and set aside until needed.

Step two Heat a wok or large frying pan over a high heat until it is very hot. Add the oil and, when it is very hot and slightly smoking, add the beef from the marinade and stir-fry for about 2 minutes. Remove the meat and drain it in a colander. Pour off all but 1¼ tablespoons of the oil and reheat it over a high heat. When it is very hot, add the onions, black beans, garlic and ginger and stir-fry for 1 minute then add the asparagus and stir-fry for 1 minute. Now add the stock or water, rice wine or sherry, sugar, 1½ teaspoons of salt and ½ teaspoon of pepper. Continue to stir-fry for 3 minutes or until the asparagus is slightly tender. Add more water as necessary.

Step three Quickly return the meat to the wok, add the oyster sauce and stir well. Turn the mixture onto a warm platter and serve at once.

Spicy Orange Lamb

Here I have combined lamb with orange to create a lovely contrast to the richness of the meat. The tartness of fresh orange zest balances the robust taste of the lamb beautifully.

Step one Cutting against the grain, cut the lamb into thin slices, 5cm (2in) long. Put the lamb in a bowl with all the marinade ingredients, mix well and leave to marinate for 20 minutes.

Step two Heat a wok or large frying pan over a high heat until it is very hot. Add the ground nut oil and, when it is very hot and slightly smoking, remove the lamb from the marinade with a slotted spoon. Add to the pan and stir-fry for 2 minutes, until the lamb browns. Remove and leave to drain in a colander or sieve set inside a bowl.

Step three Pour off all but about 2 teaspoons of the oil from the wok or pan. Reheat over a high heat and then add the ginger, garlic, orange zest and peppercorns, if using. Stir-fry for just 20 seconds.

Step four Return the lamb to the pan, add the remainder of the ingredients, season with ½ teaspoon each of salt and pepper and stir-fry for 4 minutes, mixing well. Serve at once.

Serves 4

450g (1lb) lean boneless lamb chops

3 tbsp ground nut oil

1½ tbsp finely chopped fresh root ginger

2 tbsp thinly sliced garlic

1 tbsp grated orange zest

1 tsp roasted Sichuan peppercorns, finely ground (optional)

2 tbsp orange juice

1 tbsp dark soy sauce

2 tsp chilli bean sauce

1 tsp sugar

2 tsp sesame oil

salt and pepper

for the marinade

1 tbsp light soy sauce

2 tsp Shaoxing rice wine or dry sherry

1 tsp sesame oil

2 tsp cornflour

Stir-fried Persillade Prawns

This robust seasoning gives any dish a distinctly assertive flavour.

Serves 4

450g (1lb) raw prawns

2 tbsp salt

450ml (¾ pint) ground
nut oil or water

1 tbsp extra-virgin
olive oil

for the marinade

1 egg white

2 tsp cornflour

1 tsp sesame oil

salt and white pepper

for the persillade

2 tbsp extra-virgin
olive oil

1½ tsp finely chopped
fresh root ginger

2 tbsp finely chopped
garlic

½ tsp sugar

1 tbsp finely chopped
spring onions

1 tbsp finely chopped
fresh coriander

3 tbsp finely chopped
fresh parsley

salt and pepper

Step one Peel the prawns, make a slit down the back of each one and pull out the fine digestive cord with the tip of the knife. Wash the prawns in cold water with 1 tablespoon of salt, then drain and repeat. Rinse well and pat dry with kitchen paper.

Step two Combine the prawns with all the marinade ingredients, add 1 teaspoon of salt and ½ teaspoon of white pepper, mix well and leave in the fridge for 20 minutes.

Step three Combine all the persillade ingredients in a food-processor or blender and process until finely chopped. If you are using a blender, be careful not to overblend the mixture to a purée.

Step four If using ground nut oil to cook the prawns, heat a wok or large frying pan over a high heat and then add the oil. When it is very hot, remove the wok or pan from the heat and immediately add the prawns, stirring vigorously to prevent them from sticking. When they turn white, after about 2 minutes, quickly drain the prawns in a stainless-steel colander set in a bowl. Discard the oil. If using water instead of oil, bring it to the boil in a pan, then remove from the heat and immediately add the prawns, stirring vigorously to prevent them from sticking. When the prawns turn white, after about 2 minutes, quickly drain them in a colander set in a bowl. Discard the water.

Step five If you used a wok or pan, wipe it clean. Reheat it until it is very hot, then add the olive oil. When it is hot, return the prawns to the wok and stir-fry for 20 seconds. Quickly stir in the persillade mixture and mix well. Turn onto a platter and serve at once.

Sweet and Sour Prawns

This is perhaps one of the most popular and best-known Chinese dishes in the West and is simple to make.

Step one Coarsely chop the garlic and then finely chop the root ginger. De-seed the red or green pepper and cut into 2.5cm (1in) squares, then slice the water chestnuts (if you're using fresh water chestnuts you'll need to peel them first). Heat a wok over a high heat, then add the oil. When it is very hot and slightly smoking, add the garlic, ginger and spring onions and stir-fry for around 20 seconds. Add the prawns and stir-fry them for 1 minute. Next add the pepper and water chestnuts and stir-fry for 30 seconds.

Step two Now add all the sauce ingredients except the cornflour mixture. Bring to the boil, add the cornflour mixture, then turn the heat down and simmer for 3 minutes. Serve immediately.

Serves 4

1½ tbsp garlic

2 tsp fresh root ginger

100g (4oz) red or green pepper

225g (8oz) water chestnuts

1½ tbsp ground nut oil

4 spring onions, cut into 4cm (1½in) pieces diagonally

450g (1lb) raw prawns, shelled and de-veined

for the sauce

150ml (5fl oz) home-made or good-quality bought chicken stock

2 tbsp Shaoxing rice wine or dry sherry

3 tbsp light soy sauce

2 tsp dark soy sauce

1½ tbsp tomato paste

3 tbsp Chinese white rice vinegar or cider vinegar

1 tbsp sugar

1 tbsp cornflour, blended with 2 tbsp water

For a video masterclass on chopping vegetables, go to www.mykitchentable.co.uk/videos/choppingvegetables

Spicy Sichuan-style Prawns

Sichuan cooking is popular throughout China and in recent years adventurous Chinese restaurant diners have discovered how delicious it can be. This is one of the best-known dishes from that area.

Serves 4

1½ tbsp ground nut oil

2 tsp finely chopped fresh root ginger

1 tbsp coarsely chopped garlic

2 tbsp finely chopped spring onions

450g (1lb) raw prawns, shelled and de-veined

a handful of fresh coriander sprigs, to garnish (optional)

for the sauce

1 tbsp tomato paste

2 tsp chilli bean sauce

2 tsp Chinese black vinegar or cider vinegar

2 tsp sugar

2 tsp sesame oil

salt and pepper

Step one Heat a wok over a high heat. Add the oil and, when it is very hot and slightly smoking, add the ginger, garlic and spring onions.

Step two Stir-fry for 20 seconds, then add the prawns. Stir-fry the prawns for about 1 minute.

Step three Add all the sauce ingredients, season with around ½ teaspoon each of salt and pepper and continue to stir-fry for another 3 minutes over a high heat. Serve at once, garnished with coriander sprigs, if you wish.

Hot and Sour Indonesian Prawns

Seafood is a staple of the Indonesian diet. This simple but delectable dish is typical of the cooking found in many homes. Prawns cook quickly, so they make ideal fast food. Serve with plain rice for a complete meal.

Step one Heat a wok or large frying pan over a high heat. Add the oil and, when it is very hot and slightly smoking, add the onion, garlic, ginger and chillies and stir-fry for 3 minutes.

Step two Add the cumin, coriander and shrimp paste and stir-fry for 1 minute. Now add the sugar and prawns and stir-fry for 2 minutes. Add the lemon juice, turn the heat down and simmer for 4 minutes or until most of the liquid has evaporated. Serve straight away.

Serves 4

1½ tbsp ground nut oil

1 small onion, chopped

1 tbsp finely chopped garlic

2 tsp finely chopped fresh root ginger

2 fresh red chillies, de-seeded and chopped

1 tsp ground cumin

1 ts ground coriander

1 tsp shrimp paste

1 tsp sugar

450g (1lb) raw prawns, shelled and de-veined

3 tbsp lemon juice

Prawns and Scallops in Black Bean and Tomato Butter Sauce

This makes an elegant dinner-party main, served with vegetables.

Serves 4

450g (1lb) raw prawns

salt

1½ tbsp garlic

1 tbsp salted black beans

1 tbsp fresh root ginger

2 tbsp shallots

1½ tbsp olive oil

450g (1lb) fresh scallops, including the corals

1 tbsp Shaoxing rice wine or dry sherry

1 tbsp light soy sauce

120ml (4fl oz) home-made or good-quality bought fish stock or chicken stock

175g (6oz) tomatoes, skinned and de-seeded if fresh, drained if tinned, then coarsely chopped

25g (1oz) cold unsalted butter, cut into small pieces

a handful of fresh basil leaves, cut into strips, to garnish

Step one Peel the prawns, make a slit down the back of each one and pull out the fine digestive cord with the tip of the knife. Wash the prawns in cold water with 1 tablespoon of salt, then drain and repeat. Rinse well and pat dry with kitchen paper.

Step two Coarsely chop the garlic and black beans, and finely chop the ginger and shallots. Heat a wok or large frying pan over a high heat. Add the olive oil, then the prawns and scallops, and stir-fry for 2 minutes. Remove the prawns and scallops with a slotted spoon and set aside.

Step three Add the garlic, ginger and shallots and stir-fry for 30 seconds. Then add the black beans and stir-fry for another 30 seconds. Add the rice wine or sherry, light soy sauce and stock, cover and cook over a high heat for 1 minute. Return the scallops and prawns to the wok or pan and cook for 3 minutes, until just tender. Finally, add the chopped tomatoes and, when the mixture is hot, slowly whisk in the butter a piece at a time. Turn onto a warm serving platter, garnish with the basil and serve at once.

Fragrant Prawn Curry

This is a delightful stir-fry dish. I enjoyed it for the first time in Singapore some time ago. The aromatic lemon grass gives it a unique fragrance. Prawns have a distinct but delicate taste and the clean, mildly citrus touch of the lemon grass is a perfect counterpart. Use fresh lemon grass whenever possible – if your search is fruitless, you may substitute 2 tablespoons of lemon zest.

Serves 2–4

450g (1lb) raw prawns

1 stick of lemon grass

1 fresh red or green chilli

2 tbsp ground nut oil

100g (4oz) onions, coarsely chopped

2 tbsp finely chopped garlic

2 tsp finely chopped fresh root ginger

2 tsp Madras curry paste

1 tsp chilli bean sauce

1 tsp sugar

1 tbsp Shaoxing rice wine or dry sherry

2 tsp light soy sauce

a few fresh sprigs of coriander, to garnish

salt and pepper

Step one Peel the prawns and discard the shells. Using a small sharp knife, remove the fine digestive cord. Wash the prawns in cold water with ½ teaspoon of salt, rinse well and pat them dry with kitchen paper.

Step two Remove the outer layer of the stick of lemon grass until you get to the tender, whitish core. Chop the lemon grass core finely. Split the chilli in half and carefully remove and discard the seeds. Chop the chilli finely and combine it with the lemon grass.

Step three Heat a wok or large frying pan over a high heat until it is hot. Add the oil and, when it is very hot and slightly smoking, add the onions, garlic, ginger, lemon grass and chilli and stir fry for 1 minute, then add the prawns and continue to stir-fry for 1 minute. Now add the remainder of the ingredients, season with ¼ teaspoon of pepper and add 2 tablespoons of water. Continue to stir-fry for 4 minutes or until the prawns are firm and cooked. Turn the mixture onto a warm serving platter, garnish with the coriander and serve at once.

Spicy Scallops with Sun-dried Tomatoes

Nothing is easier to stir-fry than fresh scallops, especially in a hot wok. The heat seals in all the goodness and juices. Here I have matched them with an unusual combination of sun-dried tomatoes, lemon and coriander for a light, refreshing flavour.

Serves 4

1 tbsp olive oil

2 tsp ground nut oil

450g (1lb) fresh scallops, including the corals

2 tsp finely chopped fresh root ginger

2 tbsp de-seeded and finely shredded red chillies

3 tbsp finely chopped sun-dried tomatoes

2 tsp finely grated lemon zest

1 tsp sugar

2 tbsp finely chopped fresh coriander

salt and white or black pepper

Step one Heat a wok or large frying pan over a high heat and add the olive and ground nut oils. When they are very hot and slightly smoking, add the scallops and stir-fry for 30 seconds, until lightly browned.

Step two Immediately add the ginger and chillies and stir-fry for 1 minute. Then add the sun-dried tomatoes, lemon zest, sugar and some salt and pepper and stir-fry for 2 minutes. Stir in the fresh coriander, mix well and serve at once.

Stir-fried Scallops with Mangetout

The delicate scallop requires little cooking to bring out its naturally sweet taste. Here I have combined scallops with mangetout, a delectable and toothsome vegetable that complements the scallop's sweetness. An easy dish to make, this can easily be a wonderful first course for any meal or a special treat as a main course with rice and another vegetable dish.

Step one Heat a wok or large frying pan over a high heat until it is hot. Add 1 tablespoon of oil and, when it is very hot and slightly smoking, add the ginger and spring onions and stir-fry for 10 seconds. Immediately add the scallops and stir-fry them for 1 minute then add 1 tablespoon of Shaoxing rice wine or dry sherry, the soy sauce, sugar and ½ teaspoon each of salt and white pepper. Continue to stir-fry for 2 minutes. Remove the scallops to a bowl together with the sauce and set aside.

Step two Wipe the wok clean and reheat over a high heat. When it is hot and slightly smoking, add the remaining oil and the mangetout and stir-fry for 10 seconds. Immediately add the remaining rice wine or sherry and 2 tablespoons of water and stir-fry for 2 minutes. Return the scallops to the wok and continue to stir-fry for an additional 2 minutes. Now add the sesame oil and stir-fry for another minute. Serve at once.

Serves 4

2 tbsp ground nut oil

1 tbsp finely chopped fresh root ginger

3 tbsp finely shredded spring onions

450g (1lb) scallops, including the corals

2 tbsp Shaoxing rice wine or dry sherry

2 tsp light soy sauce

1 tsp sugar

225g (8oz) mangetout, trimmed

2 tsp sesame oil

salt and white pepper

Stir-fried Fish with Black Bean Sauce

My mother loved making this dish because it was quick, easy and delicious. The pungency of the black beans, garlic and ginger turn an ordinary fish into a gourmet's delight. When served with vegetables and rice, it becomes the type of light, wholesome, satisfying meal that is the hallmark of the best Chinese home cooking.

Step one Cut the fish fillets into strips 2.5cm (1in) wide and sprinkle 2 teaspoons of salt evenly over them. Let them stand for 20 minutes.

Step two Heat a wok or large frying pan over a high heat until it is hot. Add the oil and, when it is very hot and slightly smoking, turn the heat down to medium and add the fish strips. Stir-fry these gently for about 2 minutes or until they are brown on both sides, taking care not to break them up. Remove them with a slotted spoon and drain on kitchen paper. Drain off all but 1½ tablespoons of the oil.

Step three Reheat the wok. When it is hot, add the black beans, garlic, ginger and spring onions and stir-fry for 30 seconds. Then add the soy sauces, rice wine or sherry, sugar and 1 tablespoon of water and bring to a simmer. Return the fish to the wok and gently finish cooking in the sauce for about 1 minute, then add the sesame oil and give the mixture a good stir. Using a slotted spoon, arrange the fish on a warm serving platter, garnish with the spring onions and serve at once.

Serves 4

450g (1lb) fresh, firm white fish fillets, such as cod, halibut or sea bass

3 tbsp ground nut oil

1½ tbsp coarsely chopped black beans

1 tbsp finely chopped garlic

2 tsp finely chopped fresh root ginger

3 tbsp finely chopped spring onions

1 tbsp light soy sauce

1 tsp dark soy sauce

1 tbsp Shaoxing rice wine or dry sherry

1 tsp sugar

2 tsp sesame oil

3 tbsp finely shredded spring onions, to garnish

salt

Salmon with Lemon

Once in Hong Kong, I enjoyed a salmon dish stir-fried with dried citrus peel. The tartness of the peel balanced the rich salmon nicely. I have adapted the idea by using fresh lemon, which works just as well. Fish should always be stir-fried gently, so as not to break up the very delicate flesh.

Step one Cut the salmon into strips 2.5cm (1in) wide and sprinkle 2 teaspoons of salt evenly over them. Set aside for around 20 minutes.

Step two Heat a wok or large frying pan over a high heat and add 3 tablespoons of the ground nut oil. When it is very hot and slightly smoking, turn the heat down to medium and add the salmon strips. Let them fry undisturbed for about 2 minutes, until browned, then gently turn them over to brown on the other side. Take care not to break them up. Remove with a slotted spoon and drain on kitchen paper. Wipe the wok clean.

Step three Reheat the wok and add the remaining oil then add the ginger and stir-fry for 20 seconds to brown. Now add the sugar, lemon zest, lemon segments and some salt and pepper and stir-fry gently for about 1 minute.

Step four Return the salmon to the wok and gently mix with the lemon for about 1 minute. Add the sesame oil and give the mixture a good stir. Using a slotted spoon, arrange the salmon and lemon on a warm serving platter and serve at once.

Serves 4

450g (1lb) boneless salmon fillet, skinned

4 tbsp ground nut oil

1 tbsp finely shredded fresh root ginger

1 tsp sugar

1 tbsp finely grated lemon zest

1 lemon, peeled and segmented

2 tsp sesame oil

salt and pepper

Stir-fried Squid with Vegetables

Squid cooked the Chinese way is both tender and tasty. The secret is to blanch it in boiling water, then cook it for the minimum amount of time – just enough to firm it up slightly. Cooking it for too long will make it tough, so that eating it is like chewing on rubber bands. This recipe can also be prepared with prawns if you find squid difficult to track down.

Serves 4

450g (1lb) cleaned and prepared squid

1½ tbsp ground nut oil

2 tbsp coarsely chopped garlic

1 tbsp finely chopped fresh root ginger

100g (4oz) red or green pepper, de-seeded and cut into thin strips

100g (4oz) mangetout, trimmed

3 tbsp home-made or good-quality bought chicken stock

1 tbsp Shaoxing rice wine or dry sherry

3 tbsp oyster sauce

1 tbsp light soy sauce

2 tsp dark soy sauce

2 tsp of cornflour, blended with 2 tsp water

2 tsp sesame oil

salt

Step one If the tentacles are still attached to the head of the squid, cut them off and reserve. Discard the head. Cut the squid bodies into 4cm (1½in) strips. Bring a large pan of water to the boil and then put in the strips and tentacles and blanch them by simmering them for 15 seconds. The squid will firm up slightly and turn an opaque white colour. Remove and drain in a colander.

Step two Heat a wok over a high heat, then add the oil. When it is very hot and slightly smoking, add the garlic and ginger and stir-fry for 15 seconds then add the pepper strips and mangetout and stir-fry for 1 minute.

Step three Add all the remainder of the ingredients except the squid and sesame oil and season with 2 teaspoons of salt. Bring the mixture to the boil, give it a stir, then add the squid and mix well. Cook for 30 seconds more, stir in the sesame oil and serve at once.

my KITCHEN TABLE

For step-by-step photographs of this recipe, go to www.mykitchentable.co.uk/recipes/stirfriedsquid

Stir-fried Squid with Chilli and Basil

Thai chefs are masters with seafood, especially squid. This aromatic stir-fried dish, *pla muk phat bai krapao*, is one of the simplest to cook and is flavoured with chillies, basil and garlic – a mixture that is the essence of Thai cooking. Once the squid has been prepared, the dish is only minutes away from completion. For maximum impact, delay the final cooking until the last possible moment.

Serves 4

675g (1½ lb) fresh squid (or 450g (1lb) cleaned frozen squid, thawed)

175g (6oz) fresh or frozen petits pois

1½ tbsp vegetable oil

4 tbsp coarsely chopped garlic

3 tbsp finely sliced shallots

2–3 small, fresh red Thai chillies, de-seeded and chopped

1 tbsp fish sauce (nam pla)

2 tbsp oyster sauce

2 tsp sugar

a handful of fresh Thai basil leaves or ordinary basil leaves

Step one Pull the head and tentacles of the squid away from the body; the intestines should come away with them. Then pull off the thin, purplish skin.

Step two Using a small, sharp knife, slit the body open; remove and discard the transparent bony section. Wash the body under cold running water and cut it into 4cm (1½in) strips.

Step three Slice the tentacles off the head, cutting just above the eye (you may also have to remove the polyp, or beak, from the centre of the ring of tentacles). Discard the head and reserve the tentacles.

Step four If you are using fresh peas, bring a large pan of salted water to the boil, put in the peas and blanch them for 3 minutes, then drain and set aside. If you are using frozen peas, simply thaw them and set them aside.

Step five Heat a wok or large frying pan over a high heat and add the oil. When it is very hot and slightly smoking, add the garlic and stir-fry for 1 minute, until lightly browned. Remove with a slotted spoon and drain on kitchen paper. Add the squid strips and tentacles to the wok and stir-fry for 1 minute, until beginning to turn opaque.

Step six Add the shallots, chillies, peas, fish sauce, oyster sauce and sugar and stir-fry for 3 minutes. Toss in the basil and give one last stir. Turn the mixture onto a platter, garnish with the fried garlic and serve at once.

Cantonese Crab with Black Bean Sauce

This recipe can only be made with fresh crabs in the shell, since the shell protects the delicate crabmeat during the stir-frying process. If you can't get crab in the shell, use prawns instead.

Serves 4–6

1 fresh crab in the shell, weighing about 1.5kg (3lb)

2 tbsp ground nut oil

3 tbsp coarsely chopped salted black beans

2 tbsp coarsely chopped garlic

1 tbsp finely chopped fresh root ginger

3 tbsp finely chopped spring onions

225g (8oz) minced pork

2 tbsp light soy sauce

1 tbsp dark soy sauce

2 tbsp Shaoxing rice wine or dry sherry

250ml (8fl oz) home-made or good-quality bought chicken stock

2 eggs, beaten

2 tsp sesame oil

salt

Step one To cook the crab, bring a large pot of water to the boil, add 2 teaspoons of salt and then put in the crab. Cover the pot and cook for about 5–7 minutes, until it turns bright red. Remove with a slotted spoon and drain in a colander. Leave to thoroughly cool.

Step two Place the cooked crab on its back on a board. Using your fingers, twist the claws from the body.

Step three Now twist off the bony tail flap on the underside of the crab and discard it. With your fingers, pry the body from the main shell. Remove and discard the small, bag-like stomach sac and its appendages, which are located just behind the crab's mouth.

Step four Pull the soft, feathery gills, which look a little like fingers, away from the body and discard them. Remove the legs and put to one side. Using a cleaver or heavy knife, split the crab shell in half and, using a spoon, fork or skewer, scrape out all the brown crabmeat.

Step five Using a cleaver or heavy knife, cut the crab, shell included, into large pieces. Crack the claws and legs slightly.

Step six Heat a wok over a high heat. Add the oil and, when it is very hot and slightly smoking, add the black beans, garlic, ginger and spring onions and stir-fry for 20 seconds.

Step seven Then add the pork and stir-fry for 1 minute. Add the crab pieces and all the remaining ingredients except the eggs and the sesame oil. Stir-fry over a high heat for about 10 minutes. Combine the eggs with the sesame oil and then gradually pour this into the crab mixture, stirring slowly. There should be light strands of egg trailing over the crab mixture. Turn it onto a large, warm platter, or arrange in the crab claws and serve.

Green Thai Curry Mussels

Whenever I have an unexpected crowd of friends for dinner, I naturally turn to mussels. They are easy to obtain, inexpensive and everyone has a good time eating them. Thai flavours have become so fashionable in recent years that a wide choice of green Thai curry pastes can now be found in supermarkets. This simple dish can easily be increased for larger gatherings.

Step one Scrub the mussels under cold running water, discarding any open ones that don't close when tapped lightly.

Step two Pour the coconut milk into a wok or large frying pan. Add the lime zest, curry paste, coriander, fish sauce and sugar and bring to a simmer.

Step three Add the mussels, then cover and cook for 5 minutes or until all the mussels have opened. Discard any that have difficulty opening. Give the mixture a final stir, add the basil leaves and serve at once.

Serves 4–6

1.5kg (3lb) fresh mussels

450ml (¾ pint) tinned coconut milk

1 tbsp grated lime zest

1 tbsp green Thai curry paste (or to taste)

3 tbsp chopped fresh coriander

2 tbsp fish sauce (nam pla)

1 tsp sugar

a large handful of fresh basil leaves

Stir-fried Spinach

This is the perfect way to cook vegetables such as spinach that contain a great deal of moisture. The technique is to place the spinach in a very hot wok and quickly stir-fry with some seasoning. It is that simple to prepare, and may be served hot or cold.

Serves 4

675g (1½ lb) fresh spinach

1 tbsp ground nut oil

2 tbsp coarsely chopped garlic

1 tsp sugar

salt

Step one Wash the spinach thoroughly. Remove all the stems, leaving just the leaves. Heat a wok over a high heat. Add the oil and, when it is very hot and slightly smoking, add the garlic and 1 teaspoon of salt. Stir-fry for 10 seconds.

Step two Add the spinach and stir-fry for about 2 minutes, until the leaves are thoroughly coated with the oil, garlic and salt.

Step three When the spinach has wilted to about one-third of its original size, add the sugar and stir-fry for another 4 minutes. Transfer the spinach to a plate and pour off any excess liquid. Serve immediately.

Stir-fried Broccoli

Stir-frying is one of the most appealing cooking techniques for this colourful and extraordinarily nutritious vegetable. The secret of making this simple dish is to add a little water and cover the wok tightly, so the broccoli can cook to perfection.

Step one Cut the stems off the broccoli and separate the heads into small florets. Peel and slice the stems.

Step two Heat a wok over a high heat. Add the ground nut oil and, when it is very hot and slightly smoking, add the garlic, 1 teaspoon of salt and ½ teaspoon of pepper. Stir-fry for just 30 seconds, or until the garlic is lightly browned.

Step three Add the broccoli and stir-fry for 2 minutes. Now add 6 tablespoons of water, cover tightly and cook over a high heat for around 4–5 minutes.

Step four Uncover and test the broccoli by gently piercing it with the tip of a sharp knife; it should go in quite easily. Stir in the sesame oil and stir-fry for 30 seconds, then serve.

Serves 4

450g (1lb) broccoli

1½ tbsp ground nut oil

4 garlic cloves, lightly crushed

2 tsp sesame oil

salt and pepper

Stir-fried Mixed Vegetables

The art of stir-frying vegetables is knowing when to add them to the wok. Put the tougher, more textured ones in the wok first to give them a head start. The amount of water you need to add depends on how much natural water is in the vegetables you are using. Ensure you add only the minimum amount (no more than 1–2 tablespoons) if you are using the wok covered, otherwise the vegetables become soggy.

Serves 4

225g (8oz) Chinese leaves

225g (8oz) Chinese greens, such as Chinese flowering cabbage or pak choy, or spinach

225g (8oz) asparagus

225g (8oz) carrots

1½ tbsp ground nut oil

2 tbsp coarsely chopped shallots

2 tbsp coarsely chopped garlic

2 tsp finely chopped fresh root ginger

2 tsp sugar

1 tbsp Shaoxing rice wine or dry sherry

2 tsp sesame oil

salt

Step one Cut the Chinese leaves into 4cm (1½in) strips then cut the greens and asparagus into 4cm (1½in) pieces. Cut the carrots on the diagonal into slices 5mm (¼in) thick.

Step two Heat a wok over a high heat. Add the ground nut oil and, when it is very hot and slightly smoking, add the shallots, garlic, ginger and 2 teaspoons of salt and stir-fry for 1 minute. Then add the carrots and asparagus and stir-fry for 30 seconds. Add 1–2 tablespoons of water, cover and cook over a high heat for 2 minutes.

Step three Add the Chinese leaves and greens, together with the sugar and rice wine or sherry. Stir-fry for 3 minutes or until the greens are thoroughly wilted. Then add the sesame oil and serve at once.

KITCHEN TABLE

For a video masterclass on chopping vegetables, go to www.mykitchentable.co.uk/videos/choppingvegetables

Vietnamese-style Stir-fried Vegetables

Every cuisine in the Far East has its own version of stir-fried vegetables. Here is the Vietnamese version, which shares some of the same vegetables as the Chinese one. When stir-frying vegetables, remember to begin with the firmer varieties that need more cooking.

Step one Soak the dried mushrooms in warm water for around 20 minutes, then drain them and squeeze out the excess liquid. Remove and discard the stalks and shred the caps into thin strips. Cut the Chinese leaves and cos lettuce into 4cm (1⅓in) strips, then set aside.

Step two Heat a wok or large frying pan over a high heat until it is medium hot. Add the oil, garlic and ginger and stir-fry for 1–1½ minutes, until golden brown. Now add the spring onions, dark and light soy sauce, sugar, 1 teaspoon of salt and 5 tablespoons of water, together with the mushrooms. Cook over a high heat for 2 minutes.

Step three Add the Chinese leaves and stir-fry for 5 minutes, adding a little more water if necessary. Finally, stir in the lettuce and cook for another minute. Turn the vegetables onto a platter and serve at once.

Serves 4

50g (2oz) Chinese dried mushrooms

225g (8oz) Chinese leaves

225g (8oz) cos lettuce

1 tbsp vegetable oil

2 tbsp coarsely chopped garlic

2 tsp finely chopped fresh root ginger

3 tbsp finely chopped spring onions

1 tbsp dark soy sauce

1½ tbsp light soy sauce

2 tsp sugar

salt

Rainbow Vegetables

Whoever said vegetarian food is dreary and boring had a real lack of imagination. Serve this delicious dish with noodles and hoisin sauce.

Serves 4–6

15g (½ oz) Chinese dried mushrooms

100g (4oz) carrots

100g (4oz) tinned bamboo shoots

100g (4oz) courgettes

1 red or green pepper, de-seeded

100g (4oz) celery heart

100g (4oz) pressed, seasoned beancurd

½ head iceberg lettuce

1½ tbsp ground nut oil

1 tbsp finely chopped garlic

3 tbsp finely chopped shallots

3 tbsp finely chopped spring onions

2 tsp light soy sauce

2 tsp Shaoxing rice wine or dry sherry

3 tbsp vegetarian oyster-flavoured sauce or dark soy sauce

salt and pepper

to serve

4 tbsp Hoisin sauce

Step one Soak the dried mushrooms in warm water for around 20 minutes, then drain them and squeeze out any excess liquid. Trim off the stems and shred the caps into strips 5cm (2in) long.

Step two Peel the carrots. Cut the carrots, bamboo shoots, courgettes and pepper into fine shreds 5cm (2in) long. Finely shred the celery heart and pressed bean curd. Separate and wash the lettuce leaves, spin them in a salad spinner and chill until needed.

Step three Heat a wok or large frying pan over a high heat and add the oil. When it is very hot and slightly smoking, add the finely chopped garlic, shallots and spring onions and stir-fry for 20 seconds then add the carrots and stir-fry for another minute.

Step four Add all the prepared vegetables (except the lettuce), plus the soy sauce, rice wine or sherry, oyster sauce, salt and pepper. Stir-fry the mixture for 3 minutes, then turn it out onto a platter.

Step five Arrange the lettuce leaves on a separate platter. Put the Hoisin sauce in a small bowl and serve at once.

Asparagus in Black Bean Sauce

Asparagus is such an exquisite treat that when it's in season it is worth buying as often possible. Although it isn't a traditional ingredient of southeast Asian cooking, it has been very quickly incorporated during the last few decades. With rice and perhaps one other light dish, this will make a meal for two.

Step one Heat a wok or large frying pan and add the ground nut oil. When it is hot, add the ginger, garlic and black beans and stir-fry for a few seconds.

Step two Add the chilli bean sauce and, a few seconds later, the asparagus. Stir-fry for 2 minutes.

Step three Stir in the stock, sugar and rice wine or sherry. Cook the mixture over a high heat for about 2 minutes, stirring continuously. Add the sesame oil, give the mixture a couple of stirs and serve at once.

Serves 2

1 tbsp ground nut oil

2 tsp finely chopped fresh root ginger

2 tsp finely chopped garlic

2 tbsp coarsely chopped salted black beans

2 tsp chilli bean sauce

450g (1lb) fresh asparagus, cut on the diagonal into 7.5cm (3in) lengths

150ml (¼ pint) home-made or good-quality bought vegetable stock

1 tsp sugar

3 tbsp Shaoxing rice wine or dry sherry

1 tsp sesame oil

Hong Kong-style Broccoli and Baby Corn

Innovation is a virtue in Hong Kong cuisine and the chefs there are quick to add non-traditional vegetables to their repertoire. In this recipe, we find broccoli, flown in fresh daily from California, and baby corn, flown in from Thailand. Put them together with traditional Chinese seasonings and flavourings and you have a colourful blend of East and West – so easy to prepare in your wok and serve as a side dish. If you use dark soy sauce instead of oyster sauce, this dish is perfect for vegetarians.

Serves 4

450g (1lb) broccoli (about 2 heads)

225g (8oz) baby corn

4 tbsp Chinese dried mushrooms

1½ tbsp ground nut oil

1 tsp sugar

1 tbsp Shaoxing rice wine or dry sherry

1 tbsp light soy sauce

3 tbsp oyster sauce or dark soy sauce

2 tsp sesame oil

salt and pepper

Step one Separate the broccoli into small florets, then peel and slice the stems. Bring a large pan of salted water to the boil and put in the broccoli pieces and baby corn to blanch for 3 minutes and then immerse them in cold water. Drain thoroughly.

Step two Soak the mushrooms in warm water for 20 minutes, then drain them and squeeze out the excess liquid. Remove and discard the stems and finely shred the caps.

Step three Heat a wok or large frying pan over a high heat and add the oil. When it is very hot and slightly smoking, add the broccoli, corn and mushrooms and stir-fry for 3 minutes.

Step four Add 1 teaspoon of salt and ½ teaspoon of pepper along with the sugar, rice wine or dry sherry, light soy sauce and oyster sauce or dark soy sauce and continue to stir-fry at a moderate to high heat for 2 minutes, until the vegetables are thoroughly heated through. Add the sesame oil and stir-fry for 30 seconds, then transfer to a warm platter and serve at once.

Ginger and Garlic Carrots

I find carrots that are simply boiled and slathered with butter rather boring, as do most children. No wonder they don't eat their carrots! However, when they are stir-fried in a hot wok, the carrots acquire a smoky flavour that makes them infinitely more appealing. This simple recipe will have not only children but adults asking for more.

Step one Slice the carrots thinly at a slight diagonal.

Step two Heat a wok or large frying pan over a high heat and add the oil. When it is hot, add the garlic and ginger and stir-fry for 20 seconds, until browned, then quickly add the carrots and stir-fry for 2 minutes longer. Season.

Step three Add 3–4 tablespoons of water and stir-fry for around 4 minutes or until the carrots are tender and browned. Stir in the coriander and spring onions and serve.

Serves 4

450g (1lb) carrots, peeled

1 tbsp ground nut oil

3 tbsp coarsely chopped garlic

1 tbsp finely chopped fresh root ginger

2 tbsp finely chopped fresh coriander

2 tbsp finely chopped spring onions

salt and pepper

Broad Beans with Red Curry

Buttery, succulent broad beans are a favourite throughout Asia. In Thailand they are stir-fried with red curry paste, which gives them a rich and refreshing taste without masking their distinctive qualities. This dish, called *thua pak-a-phad prig daeng*, makes an impressive and delicious side dish or starter. Broad beans are, of course, best eaten fresh, but frozen beans are an acceptable substitute.

Serves 2–4

900g (2lb) fresh broad beans, unshelled, or 350g (12oz) frozen broad beans

1 tbsp ground nut oil

3 tbsp finely sliced garlic

3 tbsp finely sliced shallots

2 small, fresh red Thai chilli peppers, de-seeded and sliced

2 tsp sugar

2 tsp Thai red curry paste

1 tbsp fish sauce (nam pla) or light soy sauce

pepper

Step one If you are using fresh broad beans, shell them and then blanch in a large pan of boiling salted water for 2 minutes. Drain thoroughly, refresh in cold water and drain again. When cool, slip off the skins. If you are using frozen beans, thaw them.

Step two Heat a wok or large frying pan over a high heat and add the oil. When it is very hot and slightly smoking, add the garlic, shallots, chilli peppers and some black pepper and stir-fry for 1 minute.

Step three Add the broad beans, sugar, red curry paste, fish sauce, 2 tablespoons of water and continue to stir-fry over a high heat for 2 minutes. Serve at once.

Bright Pepper and Green Bean Stir Fry

Red peppers and green beans, nicely seasoned, combine to form a colourful and nutritious salad that is appropriate for any meal. This dish is also good served at room temperature.

Step one Heat a wok or large frying pan and add the oil. Add the garlic, peppers, French beans and 1½ teaspoons of salt and stir-fry for 2 minutes. Then add the sugar and 2 tablespoons of water and cook for another 4 minutes or until the vegetables are tender. Serve at once.

Serves 4–6

1½ tbsp ground nut oil

2 tbsp coarsely chopped garlic

225g (8oz) red peppers, de-seeded and cut into strips

225g (8oz) French beans, trimmed

1 tsp sugar

salt

For more recipes from My Kitchen Table, sign up for our newsletter at www.mykitchentable.co.uk/newsletter

Cloud Ears Stir-fried with Mangetout

This is a colourful and wholesome vegetable dish that is easily assembled for a family dinner. It is a classic combination of the tastes and textures so typical of Chinese cookery. The cloud ears have little flavour of their own but, like mushrooms in general, they readily absorb other flavours and retain their chewy texture.

Serves 4

15g (½ oz) Chinese dried cloud ears

1 tbsp ground nut oil

2 garlic cloves, crushed

100g (4oz) celery, sliced on the diagonal

225g (8oz) mangetout, trimmed

100g (4oz) water chestnuts (peeled if fresh, rinsed if tinned), sliced

for the sauce

1 tbsp oyster sauce

1 tsp light soy sauce

2 tsp dark soy sauce

1 tsp sugar

2 tsp Shaoxing rice wine or dry sherry

2 tsp sesame oil

150ml (¼ pint) home-made or good-quality bought vegetable stock

2 tsp cornflour, blended with 2 tsp water

Step one Soak the cloud ears in warm water for 20 minutes, until soft, then drain and set aside.

Step two Heat a wok or large frying pan over a medium heat and add the oil. When hot, add the garlic and stir-fry for 30 seconds. Then add the cloud ears and celery and stir-fry for 2 minutes. Stir in the mangetout and the water chestnuts, if using fresh ones, and stir-fry for another minute.

Step three Add all the sauce ingredients except the blended cornflour. Bring the sauce to the boil and then stir in the cornflour mixture. If you are using tinned water chestnuts, add them at this stage and warm through. Turn the mixture onto a serving platter and serve at once.

Stir-fried Singapore Water Spinach

My good friend Jenny Lo, who is Malaysian–Chinese, introduced me to this delicious, earthy dish. I have since eaten it numerous times in Singapore. Water spinach is a leafy vegetable that is prolific throughout South-east Asia. It is similar to ordinary spinach, which can easily be substituted. However, the appeal of water spinach is the crunchy, hollow stalk, which is just as tasty as the leaves. You can find water spinach in Chinese supermarkets.

Step one If you are using water spinach, wash it thoroughly. Trim any tough ends off the stalks. If you are using ordinary spinach, wash it thoroughly and remove and discard the stalks.

Step two Heat a wok or large frying pan over a high heat, add the oil and, when it is very hot and slightly smoking, add the shrimp paste and crush it in the hot oil. Add the shallots and garlic and stir-fry for 2–3 minutes, until they are lightly browned.

Step three Add the chillies, sugar and spinach. Stir-fry for about 2 minutes to coat the spinach with the aromatic mixture.

Step four After the spinach has wilted to about one-third of its original size, continue to stir-fry for 4 minutes. Season with salt and pepper, transfer the spinach to a plate and pour off any excess liquid. Serve immediately.

Serves 2–4

675g (1½ lb) water spinach or ordinary spinach

2 tbsp ground nut or vegetable oil

2 tsp shrimp paste

50g (2oz) shallots, finely sliced

5 garlic cloves, finely sliced

2 fresh red chillies, de-seeded and chopped

1 tsp sugar

salt and pepper

Indonesian-style Green Bean Sambal

This is one of the tastiest recipes I know for green beans. Indonesian spicing gives it a real kick. Sambal simply means 'spice mixture', and there are many different types.

Serves 2–4

2 small, fresh red chillies, de-seeded and chopped

1 tbsp cider vinegar

1½ tbsp ground nut oil

450g (1lb) runner beans or French beans, trimmed and cut into 7.5cm (3in) lengths

2 tsp coarsely chopped garlic

1 small red onion, finely sliced

salt

Step one Place the chillies, vinegar, 1 tablespoon of water and some salt in a food-processor or blender and purée to a smooth paste, adding more water if necessary. Set aside.

Step two Heat a wok or large frying pan over a high heat until it is hot. Add the oil and, when it is very hot and slightly smoking, add the beans and stir-fry for 30 seconds.

Step three Add the puréed chilli mixture, plus the garlic, 3 tablespoons of water and some salt. Stir-fry for 1 minute.

Step four Cover the wok and cook for 5 minutes or until the beans are tender. Uncover and stir-fry until all the liquid has evaporated. Mix in the sliced red onion and serve at once.

Braised Fusion Mushrooms with Herbs

Mushrooms can turn a simple vegetarian dish into a lovely, satisfying main course such as this. In this easy recipe for a mushroom stew, I combine Chinese dried mushrooms, which have a rich, smoky flavour, with button mushrooms and dried morel mushrooms.

Step one Soak the dried Chinese and morel mushrooms in two separate bowls of warm water for 20 minutes then drain the Chinese mushrooms and squeeze out the excess liquid. Strain this mushroom liquid and reserve. Remove and discard the mushroom stems and cut the caps in half. Rinse the morel mushrooms, to remove any sand. Slice the button mushrooms.

Step two Heat a wok or large frying pan over a high heat until it is moderately hot. Add the oil and immediately add the garlic and stir-fry for 15 seconds. Then add 2 teaspoons of salt, 1 teaspoon of pepper and all the mushrooms with the mushroom liquid and stir-fry them for 2 minutes. Add the rice wine or sherry, soy sauce and sugar and continue stir-frying for 5 minutes or until the mushroom liquid has been re-absorbed by the mushrooms or evaporated.

Step three Finally, add the cream and cook for 2 minutes. Give the mushrooms a few stirs, turn onto a warm platter, sprinkle with chives and spring onions and serve at once.

Serves 2–4

50g (2oz) Chinese dried black mushrooms

50g (2oz) dried morel mushrooms

900g (2lb) button mushrooms

3 tbsp extra-virgin olive oil

4 tbsp coarsely chopped garlic

4 tbsp Shaoxing rice wine or dry sherry

4 tsp light soy sauce

2 tsp sugar

50ml (2fl oz) double cream

salt and pepper

to garnish

2 tbsp finely snipped fresh chives

2 tbsp finely chopped spring onions

Easy Mangetout and Sweet Water Chestnuts

Paired with the sweet crunchiness of the fresh water chestnuts, and the contrasting texture and distinct flavour of Chinese black mushrooms, mangetout make a refreshing change to ordinary peas, carrots, onions and whatever. With your wok, they take but minutes to cook and, as a side dish, nicely complement any meat or chicken.

Serves 4

225g (8oz) fresh or tinned (drained weight) water chestnuts

50g (2oz) Chinese black mushrooms

1 tbsp ground nut oil

3 tbsp finely chopped spring onions

225g (8oz) mangetout, trimmed

1 tbsp light soy sauce

1 tbsp Shaoxing rice wine or dry sherry

2 tbsp dark soy sauce

1 tsp sugar

2 tsp sesame oil

salt and pepper

Step one If you are using fresh water chestnuts, peel them. If you are using tinned water chestnuts, drain them well and rinse in cold water. Thinly slice the water chestnuts. Soak the mushrooms in warm water for 20 minutes. Drain them and squeeze out the excess liquid. Remove and discard the stems and finely shred the caps into thin strips.

Step two Heat a wok or large frying pan over a high heat until it is hot. Add the oil and, when it is very hot and slightly smoking, add the spring onions and stir-fry for 10 seconds. Add the mangetout, mushrooms and fresh water chestnuts, if you are using them, and stir-fry for 1 minute. Ensure you coat them thoroughly with the oil.

Step three Add 3 tablespoons of water and the remaining ingredients, except the sesame oil, and season with 1 teaspoon of salt and ½ teaspoon of pepper. Continue to stir-fry for another 3 minutes. If you are using tinned water chestnuts, add these now and cook for a final 2 minutes or until the vegetables are cooked. Stir in the sesame oil, transfer to a warm platter and serve at once.

Rich Aubergine with Tomato and Basil

This savoury treat combines two of my favourite vegetables, aubergines and tomatoes. The smaller, long, thin Chinese aubergines are preferable to the thicker European variety because of their slightly sweeter and milder taste. However, you may use the European type. Leave the skins of the aubergines on as they enhance the texture of the dish.

Step one Cut the aubergines into diagonal slices around 1cm (½in) thick.

Step two If you are using fresh tomatoes, bring a large pan of water to the boil and then plunge them in and cook for a few seconds, removing them with a slotted spoon. Then peel, de-seed and cut them into 2.5cm (1in) chunks. If you are using tinned tomatoes, chop them into small chunks.

Step three Heat a wok or large frying pan over a high heat until it is hot. Add the oil and, when it is moderately hot, add the garlic and stir-fry for 30 seconds then add the aubergine slices, 2 teaspoons of salt and ½ teaspoons of pepper and continue to stir-fry for 2 minutes.

Step four Add the tomatoes and sugar to the aubergine and continue to cook for 5 minutes. Turn the heat down to low, cover and cook slowly for 15 minutes until the aubergine is quite tender. Stir in the basil leaves and lemon juice and give the mixture several good stirs. Transfer to a warm platter and serve at once or allow to cool and serve at room temperature.

Serves 4

450g (1lb) Chinese aubergines or ordinary aubergines, trimmed

225g (8oz) fresh or tinned tomatoes

75ml (3fl oz) extra-virgin olive oil

6 garlic cloves, peeled and crushed

2 tsp sugar

3 tbsp finely chopped basil leaves

1 tbsp lemon juice

salt and pepper

For Ken Hom's guide to ingredients, go to
www.mykitchentable.co.uk/authors/KenHom/ingredients

Sweet and Sour Onions

The wok is ideal for preparing this delicious vegetable recipe. These sweet and sour onions are a simple food that will proudly complement any main course. The onions are stir-fried in the wok, then allowed to cool in the sauce. The result is a delicious relish for any meats or fish or it can be served as part of a tasty vegetarian meal. Try to get the red onions which are sometimes a bit sweeter.

Serves 4–6

450g (1lb) red or yellow onions, cut into 2.5cm (1in) thick slices

1 tbsp ground nut oil

2 tbsp coarsely chopped garlic

1 tbsp dark soy sauce

2 tbsp black or red rice vinegar

2 tbsp sugar

salt

Step one Heat a wok or large frying pan over a high heat until it is hot. Add the oil and, when it is very hot and slightly smoking, add the garlic and stir-fry for 20 seconds, then add the onions and ½ teaspoon of salt. Continue to stir-fry for 1 minute.

Step two Now add the soy sauce, vinegar and sugar and continue to cook for 3 minutes, until it is well mixed. Turn the mixture onto a platter, allow it to cool and then chill for at least 1 hour so it is well chilled before serving.

Spicy Pomelo Salad

Pomelos are available in Asian and Chinese supermarkets but if you can't find them, use two grapefruit instead – white grapefruit for tartness or ruby red for a milder, sweeter taste.

Step one Gently break the pomelo segments into pieces and place in a large bowl. Heat a wok or large frying pan and add the oil. When it is hot, add the shallots and garlic and stir-fry until golden brown. Remove and drain on kitchen paper.

Step two Add the browned shallots and garlic to the pomelo, then add the chillies, peanuts, spring onions and dried shrimp and gently mix together.

Step three Combine the lime juice, fish sauce and sugar in a small bowl. Pour this over the pomelo mixture and toss carefully. Garnish with the coriander leaves, arrange on a platter and serve at once.

Serves 4

1 large pomelo, peeled and separated into segments, removing any skin or membrane

2 tbsp vegetable oil

3 tbsp finely sliced shallots

3 tbsp finely sliced garlic

2 small, fresh red Thai chillies, de-seeded and chopped

3 tbsp chopped roasted peanuts

3 tbsp finely shredded spring onions

2 tbsp chopped dried shrimp

2 tbsp lime juice

1 tbsp fish sauce (nam pla)

1 tbsp sugar

a handful of fresh coriander leaves, to garnish

Egg-fried Rice

Egg fried rice is common in Chinese restaurants and is probably the best-known Chinese dish in the West. The secret is to use cold cooked rice and a very hot wok. Remember that authentic fried rice should have a wonderful smoky taste, and should never be greasy or heavy.

Serves 4

enough long-grain rice to fill a glass measuring jug to 400ml (14fl oz)

2 large eggs, lightly beaten

2 tsp sesame oil

2 tbsp ground nut oil

2 tbsp finely chopped spring onions

salt and pepper

Step one At least 2 hours in advance, or the night before, cook the rice according to the packet instructions. Spread it out on a baking sheet and allow it to cool thoroughly, then put it in the fridge until needed.

Step two Put the eggs, sesame oil and ½ teaspoon of salt in a small jug or bowl, mix with a fork and set aside.

Step three Heat a wok over a high heat. Add the ground nut oil and, when it is very hot and slightly smoking, add the cold cooked rice. Stir-fry for 3 minutes, or until it is heated through.

Step four Next drizzle in the egg and oil mixture and continue to stir-fry for 2–3 minutes or until the eggs have set and the mixture is dry.

Step five Add ½ teaspoon of salt and ¼ teaspoon of pepper and stir-fry for 2 minutes longer, then toss in the spring onions. Stir several times, turn onto a platter and serve at once.

Chicken Fried Rice with Basil

Fried rice in all its forms is a favourite in Thailand. *Khao phad gai horapa* is one of the most popular versions, made with chicken and fragrant basil. Use Thai jasmine rice, if possible, as its aroma adds so much to the dish.

Step one At least 2 hours in advance, or the night before, cook the rice according to the packet instructions. Spread it out on a baking sheet and allow it to cool thoroughly, then put it in the fridge until needed.

Step two Slice the chicken into thin strips and set aside. Heat a wok or large frying pan over a high heat and add the oil. When it is very hot and slightly smoking, add the garlic, onion, shallots, chillies, 2 teaspoons of salt and ½ teaspoon of pepper and stir-fry for 2 minutes.

Step three Add the chicken and stir fry for 3 minutes, then add the rice and continue to stir-fry for 3 minutes. Add the sugar and fish sauce and stir-fry for 2 minutes.

Step four Finally, add the basil leaves and stir-fry for another minute. Turn onto a platter, garnish with the spring onions and serve hot – or leave to cool and serve as a rice salad.

Serves 4–6

enough dried Thai jasmine rice or long grain white rice to fill a measuring jug to 400ml (14fl oz)

225g (8oz) boneless skinless chicken breasts

2 tbsp vegetable oil

3 tbsp finely sliced garlic

1 small onion, finely chopped

3 tbsp sliced shallots

100g (4oz) large, fresh red chillies, de-seeded and shredded

2 tsp sugar

1 tbsp fish sauce (nam pla)

a handful of fresh Thai basil leaves or ordinary basil leaves

3 tbsp finely shredded spring onions

salt and pepper

Vegetarian Fried Rice

Buddhism is a powerful force in Thai culture. For one week in autumn, Thais celebrate by eating only vegetables to purify both body and soul. *Khao phad jay* is typical of the vegetarian dishes enjoyed during this popular festival.

Serves 4–6

enough dried long grain white rice to fill a measuring jug to 400ml (14fl oz)

2 tbsp vegetable oil

3 tbsp coarsely chopped garlic

1 small onion, finely chopped

175g (6oz) runner beans or French beans, diced

100g (4oz) fresh or frozen sweetcorn

2 tbsp light soy sauce

2 tsp Thai green curry paste

pepper

to garnish

3 spring onions

1 cucumber

1 lime

Step one At least 2 hours in advance, or the night before, cook the rice according to the packet instructions. Spread it out on a baking sheet and allow it to cool thoroughly, then put it in the fridge until needed.

Step two Prepare the garnishes. Cut the spring onions on a slight diagonal into 2.5cm (1in) lengths. Peel the cucumber, then slice it in half lengthways and remove the seeds with a teaspoon. Cut the cucumber into very thin slices. Cut the lime into wedges. Set aside.

Step three Heat a wok or large frying pan over a high heat and add the oil. When it is very hot and slightly smoking, add the garlic, onion and ½ teaspoon of pepper and stir-fry for 2 minutes. Then add the beans and sweetcorn and continue to stir-fry for 3 minutes.

Step four Add the cold cooked rice and stir-fry for 5 minutes. Finally, add the light soy sauce and curry paste and stir-fry for 2 minutes. Turn onto a platter, garnish with the spring onions, cucumber slices and lime wedges and serve at once.

Indonesian Fried Rice

This is the famous Indonesian *nasi goreng* – a truly delectable one-meal rice dish that is made simply in a wok. Unlike the Chinese version of fried rice, it includes a combination of meat and prawns. Soy sauce and shrimp paste are also added, which is uniquely Indonesian. It is typical of the rich and flavourful food found in Indonesia.

Step one At least 2 hours in advance, or the night before, cook the rice according to the packet instructions. Spread it out on a baking sheet and allow it to cool thoroughly, then put it in the fridge until needed.

Step two Combine the eggs with the sesame oil, ½ teaspoon of salt and some pepper, then set aside.

Step three Heat a wok or large frying pan over a high heat. Add the oil and, when it is very hot and slightly smoking, add the garlic, prawns, onion, shrimp paste, ½ teaspoon of salt and some pepper. Stir-fry for 2 minutes.

Step four Add the minced pork or beef and stir-fry for 2 minutes. Now add the rice and continue to stir-fry for 3 minutes. Next, add the light soy sauce and dark soy sauce and stir-fry for 2 minutes.

Step five Add the egg mixture and stir-fry for another minute. Turn onto a platter, garnish with the sliced cucumber and serve at once.

Serves 4–6

enough dried long grain white rice to fill a measuring jug to 400ml (14fl oz)

2 eggs, beaten

2 tsp sesame oil

2 tbsp ground nut oil

2 tbsp coarsely chopped garlic

175g (6oz) raw prawns, shelled and de-veined, then cut into 1cm (½ in) pieces

1 small onion, finely chopped

1 tbsp shrimp paste

225g (8oz) minced pork or beef

1 tbsp light soy sauce

2 tsp dark soy sauce

1 small cucumber, peeled and finely sliced

salt and pepper

Sweetcorn and Ginger Fried Rice

Sweetcorn and rice go well together, with their contrasting and complementary textures, colours and flavours. The addition of ginger makes them a little exotic – a true East–West delight. Use fresh corn if possible, and ensure the cooked rice is cold before stir-frying. This will prevent it absorbing too much oil and becoming sticky. This economical and healthy dish may be eaten as a rice salad or as an accompaniment to other foods.

Serves 4

enough dried Basmati rice to fill a measuring jug to 400ml (14fl oz)

450g (1lb) fresh corn on the cob, or 275g (10oz) tinned sweetcorn

1 tbsp ground nut oil

1½ tbsp finely chopped fresh root ginger

2 tbsp finely chopped spring onions

2 tbsp Shaoxing rice wine or dry sherry

2 tbsp sesame oil

salt and pepper

Step one At least 2 hours in advance, or even the night before, cook the rice according to the packet instructions. Spread it out on a baking sheet and allow it to cool thoroughly and then chill in the fridge.

Step two If using fresh corn, remove the kernels with a sharp knife or cleaver. You should end up with about 275g (10oz) corn. If you are using tinned corn, empty it into a sieve, drain well and set aside.

Step three Heat a wok or large frying pan and add the ground nut oil. Put in the ginger and spring onions and stir-fry for a few seconds. Add the rice wine or sherry and stir-fry for a few seconds longer.

Step four Stir in the cold cooked rice and stir-fry for 5 minutes, then add the corn and ¼ teaspoon each of salt and pepper and stir-fry for 2 minutes. Finally, add the sesame oil and stir-fry for a further 4 minutes until the corn is thoroughly cooked. Serve at once, or leave to cool and serve as a rice salad.

Classic Thai Fried Rice

Fried rice is found everywhere in Thailand. It is often served with a fried egg on top, which makes it a meal on its own. Its Thai name is *khao phad ruam mit.*

Step one At least 2 hours in advance, or the night before, cook the rice according to the packet instructions. Spread it out on a baking sheet and allow it to cool thoroughly, then chill in the fridge until needed.

Step two Beat the eggs with the sesame oil and ½ teaspoon of salt and set aside. Cut the chicken into 1cm (½in) dice.

Step three Heat a wok or large frying pan over a high heat and add the oil. When it is very hot and slightly smoking, add the garlic, onion and ½ teaspoon of pepper and stir-fry for 2 minutes. Then add the chicken and stir-fry for another 2 minutes. Add the cold cooked rice and continue to stir-fry for 3 minutes.

Step four Add the fish sauce, spring onions, coriander and chillies and stir-fry for 2 minutes.

Step five Finally, add the egg mixture and continue to stir-fry for another minute. Turn onto a platter, garnish with the lime wedges and the fried eggs, if using, and serve at once.

Serves 4-6

enough dried long grain white rice to fill a measuring jug to 400ml (14fl oz)

2 eggs, beaten

2 tsp sesame oil

225g (8oz) boneless skinless chicken breasts

2 tbsp vegetable oil

2 tbsp coarsely chopped garlic

1 small onion, finely chopped

3 tbsp fish sauce (nam pla)

3 tbsp finely chopped spring onions

3 tbsp finely chopped fresh coriander

2 small, fresh red or green Thai chillies, de-seeded and chopped

salt and pepper

to garnish

1 lime, cut into wedges

4 fried eggs (optional)

Herbal Fried Rice

Often when I cook at home, I have bits of all sorts of fresh herbs left over and I've found that adding them to cooked rice is an economical, delicious and quick way to use them up. The result is a wonderfully aromatic and fragrant rice dish.

Serves 4–6

enough dried Basmati rice to fill a measuring jug to 400ml (14fl oz)

3 tbsp extra-virgin olive oil

3 tbsp coarsely chopped garlic

2 tsp finely chopped fresh root ginger

3 tbsp finely chopped spring onions

3 tbsp finely snipped fresh chives

3 tbsp finely chopped fresh coriander

1 tbsp finely chopped fresh tarragon

2 tsp finely chopped fresh thyme

3 tbsp finely chopped fresh parsley

3 tbsp chopped fresh basil

salt and pepper

Step one At least 2 hours in advance, or the night before, cook the rice according to the packet instructions. Spread it out on a baking sheet and allow it to cool thoroughly, then put it in the fridge until needed.

Step two Heat a wok or large frying pan and add the oil. Add the garlic and ginger and stir-fry for 15 seconds. Then add the cold rice, 2 teaspoons of salt and 1 teaspoon of pepper and stir-fry for 2 minutes over a high heat. Mix well, pressing on the cold rice to break up any lumps.

Step three When the rice is heated through, add the spring onions and all the fresh herbs and stir-fry for 3 minutes. Transfer onto a serving platter and serve hot or at room temperature.

Have you made this recipe? Tell us what you think at
www.mykitchentable.co.uk/blog

148

Stir-fried Rice Noodles

Phad thai is probably one of the most popular dishes in Thailand, prepared in homes throughout the country.

Step one Soak the rice noodles in a bowl of warm water for 25 minutes, then drain them in a colander or sieve.

Step two Heat a wok or large frying pan over a high heat until it is very hot, then add 1 tablespoon of the oil. When it is very hot and slightly smoking, add the prawns and stir-fry for about 2 minutes. Remove from the pan and set aside.

Step three Reheat the wok, add the remaining oil, then add the garlic, shallots and chillies and stir-fry for 1 minute. Now add the drained noodles and stir-fry for another minute. Finally, add the beaten eggs, lime juice, fish sauce, chilli sauce, sugar and ¼ teaspoon of pepper and continue to stir fry for 3 minutes.

Step four Return the prawns to the wok, toss in the beansprouts and stir-fry for 2 minutes. Turn the mixture onto a platter. Coarsely chop the coriander and peanuts, and slice the spring onions. Garnish the platter with the lime wedges, coriander, spring onions, peanuts and chilli flakes and serve at once.

Serves 4

225g (8oz) wide dried rice noodles

3 tbsp vegetable oil

450g (1lb) raw prawns, shelled and de-veined

3 tbsp coarsely chopped garlic

3 tbsp finely sliced shallots

2 large, fresh red or green chillies, de-seeded and chopped

2 eggs, beaten

2 tbsp lime juice

3 tbsp fish sauce (nam pla)

1 tbsp sweet chilli sauce

1 tsp sugar

175g (6oz) beansprouts

pepper

to garnish

3 tbsp fresh coriander

3 tbsp roasted peanuts

3 spring onions

1 lime, cut into wedges

1 tsp dried chilli flakes

Chow Mein

Chow mein is a quick and delicious way to prepare egg noodles.

Serves 4

225g (8oz) dried or fresh egg noodles

4 tsp sesame oil

100g (4oz) boneless skinless chicken breasts, cut into fine shreds 5cm (2in) long

2½ tbsp ground nut oil

1 tbsp finely chopped garlic

50g (2oz) mangetout, finely shredded

50g (2oz) Parma ham or cooked ham, finely shredded

2 tsp light soy sauce

2 tsp dark soy sauce

1 tbsp Shaoxing rice wine or dry sherry

½ tsp sugar

3 tbsp finely chopped spring onions

salt and white pepper

for the marinade

2 tsp light soy sauce

2 tsp Shaoxing rice wine or dry sherry

1 tsp sesame oil

salt and white pepper

Step one Bring a large pan of salted water to the boil and put the noodles in to cook for 3–5 minutes, then drain and plunge them in cold water. Drain thoroughly, toss them with 3 teaspoons of the sesame oil and set aside.

Step two Combine the chicken shreds with all the marinade ingredients and season with ½ teaspoon each of salt and white pepper. Mix well and then leave to marinate for 10 minutes.

Step three Heat a wok over a high heat. Add 1 tablespoon of the ground nut oil and, when it is very hot and slightly smoking, add the chicken shreds. Stir-fry for about 2 minutes and then transfer to a plate. Wipe the wok clean. Reheat the wok until it is very hot, then add the remaining ground nut oil. When the oil is slightly smoking, add the garlic and stir-fry for 10 seconds. Then add the mangetout and ham and stir-fry for about 1 minute.

Step four Add the noodles, soy sauces, rice wine or sherry, sugar, spring onions, 1 teaspoon of salt and ½ teaspoon of white pepper. Stir-fry for 2 minutes.

Singapore Noodles

These light and subtle rice noodles are ideal for the spicy sauce.

Step one Soak the rice noodles in a bowl of warm water for 25 minutes, then drain them in a colander or sieve. In a small bowl, combine the eggs with the sesame oil, 1 teaspoon of salt and ½ teaspoon of pepper and set aside. Soak the dried mushrooms in warm water for 20 minutes, then drain them and squeeze out the excess liquid. Remove and discard the stalks and shred the caps into thin strips.

Step two Coarsely chop the garlic and finely chop the ginger. De-seed and finely shred the chillies, then slice the water chestnuts (if you're using fresh water chestnuts you'll need to peel them first). Finely shred the spring onions and, finally, shred the cooked ham and shell the prawns. Heat a wok over a high heat, then add the ground nut oil. When it is very hot and slightly smoking, add the garlic, ginger and chillies and stir-fry for 30 seconds. Add the water chestnuts, mushrooms, ham and spring onions and stir fry for 1 minute. Then add the rice noodles, prawns and peas and stir-fry for another 2 minutes.

Step three Add all the sauce ingredients, season with 1 teaspoon each of salt and pepper and cook over a high heat for 5 minutes or until most of the liquid has evaporated.

Step four Now pour the egg mixture over the noodles and stir-fry constantly until the egg has set. Turn the noodles onto a large platter, garnish with coriander leaves and serve at once.

Serves 6–8

225g (8oz) thin dried rice noodles

2 eggs, beaten

1 tbsp sesame oil

50g (2oz) Chinese black mushrooms

1¼ tbsp garlic

1 tbsp fresh root ginger

6 fresh red chillies

6 water chestnuts

3 spring onions

100g (4oz) cooked ham

100g (4oz) cooked small prawns

3 tbsp ground nut oil

175g (6oz) frozen peas, thawed

fresh coriander leaves, to garnish

salt and pepper

for the curry sauce

2 tbsp light soy sauce

3 tbsp Madras curry paste or powder

2 tbsp Shaoxing rice wine or dry sherry

1 tbsp sugar

250ml (8fl oz) tinned coconut milk

175ml (6fl oz) home-made or good-quality bought chicken stock

Spicy Sichuan Noodles

This is a typical Sichuan dish. Although it is spicy and pungent, it is nevertheless popular throughout China, especially in the north.

Serves 4

225g (8oz) minced fatty pork

450g (1lb) dried or fresh Chinese egg noodles

1 tbsp sesame oil

2 tbsp garlic

2 tbsp fresh root ginger

5 tbsp spring onions

2 tbsp ground nut oil

2 tbsp sesame paste or smooth peanut butter

2 tbsp dark soy sauce

2 tsp light soy sauce

2 tsp chilli bean sauce

2 tbsp chilli oil

250ml (8fl oz) home-made or good-quality bought chicken stock

2 tsp Sichuan peppercorns, roasted and ground

salt and pepper

for the marinade

1 tbsp dark soy sauce

2 tsp Shaoxing rice wine or dry sherry

salt and pepper

Step one Combine the pork with all the marinade ingredients in a bowl and mix well. Leave to marinate for 20 minutes.

Step two Bring a large pan of salted water to the boil and put in the noodles to cook for 3–5 minutes, then drain and plunge them into cold water. Drain thoroughly and toss them in the sesame oil. (They can be kept in this state, tightly covered with clingfilm, for up to 2 hours in the refrigerator.)

Step three Finely chop the garlic, ginger and spring onions. Heat a wok or large frying pan until it is very hot and add the ground nut oil. When it is very hot and slightly smoking, add the garlic, ginger and spring onions and stir-fry for 30 seconds. Then add the pork mixture and continue to stir-fry until the pork loses its pink colour.

Step four Add all the remaining ingredients except the Sichuan peppercorns and cook for 2 minutes. Now add the noodles, mixing well. Turn the mixture onto a warm serving platter, sprinkle with the ground peppercorns and serve at once.

Stir-fried Vegetables over a Rice Noodle Cloud

Practically any stir-fried dish with a little sauce makes a wonderful topping for these crisp, crackling, crunchy noodles. In this recipe, I combine them with slightly spiced vegetables, enhanced with aromatic seasonings.

Step one Cut the aubergines and courgettes into 7.5cm (3in) batons. Sprinkle them with salt and leave in a sieve to drain for 20 minutes. Rinse under cold running water and pat dry with kitchen paper.

Step two Heat the oil in a deep-fat fryer or large wok. Add the noodles and deep-fry until they are crisp and puffed up. Remove with a slotted spoon and drain on kitchen paper. You may have to do this in several batches.

Step three Heat a wok or large frying pan and add 1½ tablespoons of the oil in which you fried the noodles. When moderately hot, crush and add the garlic along with the chopped spring onions and stir-fry for 30 seconds. Add the aubergines and courgettes and continue to stir-fry for 1 minute.

Step four Stir in all the remainder of the ingredients except the cornflour mixture, season with 1 teaspoon of salt and cook for 3 minutes. Finally, add the blended cornflour and cook for a minute longer. Place the deep-fried noodles on a platter and spoon the vegetables over the top. Serve immediately.

Serves 4–6

350g (12oz) aubergines

225g (8oz) courgettes

300ml (½ pint) ground nut oil

175g (6oz) rice noodles, rice vermicelli or rice sticks

3 garlic cloves

4 spring onions, chopped

2 tbsp Shaoxing rice wine or dry sherry

2 tbsp yellow bean sauce

2 tsp chilli bean sauce

150ml (¼ pint) home-made or good-quality bought chicken stock or vegetable stock

1 tsp sugar

2 tbsp dark soy sauce

1 tsp cornflour, blended with 1 tsp water

salt

Curry Rice Noodles with Vegetables

This is a vegetarian version of the popular dish Singapore noodles.

Serves 4–6

225g (8oz) rice noodles

50g (2oz) Chinese dried mushrooms

225g (8oz) frozen petit pois

225g (8oz) Chinese leaves

3 tbsp ground nut oil

3 tbsp finely sliced garlic

1 tbsp finely chopped fresh root ginger

6 fresh red or green chillies, de-seeded and finely shredded

6 water chestnuts (peeled if fresh, rinsed if tinned), sliced

3 spring onions, finely shredded

salt and white pepper

fresh coriander leaves, to garnish

for the curry sauce

2 tbsp light soy sauce

3 tbsp Madras curry powder

2 tbsp Shaoxing rice wine or dry sherry

1 tbsp sugar

400ml (14fl oz) tinned coconut milk

salt and pepper

Step one Soak the rice noodles in a bowl of warm water for 25 minutes and then drain them in a colander or sieve.

Step two Soak the mushrooms in warm water for 20 minutes then drain them and squeeze out the excess liquid. Remove and discard the stems and finely shred the caps into thin strips.

Step three Put the peas in a small bowl and let them thaw. Finely shred the Chinese leaves. Heat a wok or large frying pan over a high heat until it is hot. Add the oil and, when it is very hot and slightly smoking, add the garlic, ginger and chillies and stir-fry the mixture for 30 seconds then add the water chestnuts, mushrooms, Chinese leaves, spring onions, 1 teaspoon of salt and ½ teaspoon of white pepper and stir-fry for 1 minute. Then add the rice noodles and peas and continue to stir-fry for 2 minutes.

Step four Now add all the sauce ingredients and season with ½ teaspoon each of salt and pepper, then continue to cook over a high heat for another 5 minutes or until most of the liquid has evaporated. Turn the noodles onto a large warm platter, garnish with the coriander leaves and serve at once.

Angel Hair Pasta with Spicy Tomato Sauce

Chinese noodles are made from a softer wheat than Italian pasta. However, I love the al dente texture of pasta. Here I have added a spicy twist to this classic Italian dish with a few Asian flavours.

Step one If you are using fresh tomatoes, skin and de-seed them, then cut them into 2.5cm (1in) cubes. If you are using tinned tomatoes, cut them into small chunks.Heat a wok or large frying pan and add the oil. Add the onions, ginger, garlic, spring onions and chilli peppers and stir-fry for 2 minutes. Then add the chilli bean sauce, rice wine or sherry, sugar, 2 teaspoons of salt and 1 teaspoon of pepper and continue to cook for 1 minute.

Step two Add the tomatoes, turn down the heat to low and simmer gently for 30 minutes. The sauce can be made a day ahead to this point.

Step three Bring a large pan of salted water to the boil and put in the pasta to cook according to the packet instructions until al dente. Drain well and add to the sauce in the wok. Mix thoroughly, stir in the basil leaves and serve on a large platter, with freshly grated Parmesan.

Serves 4–6

900g (2lb) fresh or tinned tomatoes

150ml (¼ pint) extra-virgin olive oil

100g (4oz) onions, finely chopped

2 tbsp finely chopped fresh root ginger

3 tbsp coarsely chopped garlic

2 tbsp finely chopped spring onions

2 tbsp de-seeded and finely chopped red chilli peppers

1 tbsp chilli bean sauce

1 tbsp Shaoxing rice wine or dry sherry

2 tsp sugar

450g (1lb) dried angel hair pasta

salt and pepper

to serve

a small handful of fresh basil leaves

freshly grated Parmesan

Stir-fried Fusilli alla Carbonara

Stir-frying is a quick and easy way to turn leftovers in your fridge into a delicious and tasty treat. Simply add cooked Italian pasta to the mix and you have a satisfying meal. In this recipe I have added bacon as well as eggs to make my version of pasta *alla carbonara*, without the cream. This recipe makes a fine starter for a multi-course meal or can easily be a main course with salad.

Serves 4

350g (12oz) dried fusilli

3 tbsp olive oil

3 tbsp coarsely chopped garlic

1 small onion, chopped

2 tbsp finely grated orange zest

12 thin slices of pancetta (or 12 bacon rashers), chopped

2 large eggs, beaten

a handful of snipped fresh chives, chopped

salt and pepper

Step one Bring a large pan of salted water to the boil and put in the pasta to cook until al dente, then drain well and set aside.

Step two Heat a wok or large frying pan over a high heat and add the oil. When it is very hot and slightly smoking, add the garlic, onion and orange zest and stir-fry for 2 minutes. Then add the pancetta or bacon and stir-fry for 3–4 minutes, until browned.

Step three Next, add the drained pasta and some salt and pepper and stir-fry for 5 minutes over a high heat. Add the beaten eggs and stir-fry until the bits of egg have set. Give the mixture a good stir and turn onto a large platter. Garnish abundantly with the chives and serve at once.

Stir-fried Pasta with Orange and Curry

I find that one of the easiest ways to prepare Italian pasta is in the wok.

Step one Cook the pasta in a large pan of salted water, according to the packet instructions. Drain well and set aside.

Step two Heat a wok or large frying pan over a high heat until it is hot. Add the oil and, when it is very hot and slightly smoking, add the garlic, ginger, onion and orange zest and stir-fry for 2 minutes then add the bacon and continue to stir-fry for 3–4 minutes or until the bacon is browned. Next add the peppers, sugar, stock, tomatoes, curry paste, tomato purée, 1 teaspoon of salt and ¼ teaspoon of pepper. Turn the heat down, cover and simmer for 30 minutes.

Step three Add the drained pasta and mix well in the wok. Turn the mixture out onto a large, warm platter, garnish abundantly with plenty of basil and chives and serve at once.

Serves 4

450g (1lb) dried
Italian pasta, such as
fusilli or farfalle

3 tbsp olive oil

3 tbsp coarsely
chopped garlic

1 tbsp finely chopped
fresh root ginger

1 small onion,
chopped

2 tbsp finely chopped
orange zest

6 bacon rashers,
rinded and chopped

225g (8oz) red pepper,
de-seeded and cut
into 1cm (½in) dice

225g (8oz) yellow
pepper, de-seeded
and cut into 1cm (½in)
dice

2 tsp sugar

300ml (½ pint) home-
made or good-quality
bought chicken stock

400g (14oz) tin
chopped tomatoes

3 tbsp Madras curry
paste

2 tbsp tomato purée

salt and pepper

to garnish

chopped fresh basil

snipped fresh chives

Spicy Noodle Salad

Yam woon sen is one of many culinary delights found in night markets throughout Thailand and can be cooked in the wok in a matter of minutes. It is often served at room temperature.

Serves 4

225g (8oz) flat rice noodles, rice vermicelli or rice sticks

1 tbsp vegetable oil

3 tbsp chopped dried shrimp

3 tbsp sliced garlic

3 tbsp sliced shallots

225g (8oz) minced pork

3 tbsp fish sauce (nam pla)

1 tbsp sugar

3 tbsp lime juice

3–4 small, fresh red or green Thai chillies, de-seeded and chopped

salt and pepper

to garnish

50g (2oz) roasted peanuts, crushed

a handful of fresh coriander sprigs

Step one Soak the rice noodles in a bowl of warm water for 25 minutes, then drain them in a colander or sieve.

Step two Heat a wok or large frying pan over a high heat and add the oil. When it is very hot and slightly smoking, add the dried shrimp and garlic and stir-fry for 1 minute, until golden brown. Then add the shallots and pork and stir-fry for 3 minutes.

Step three Now add the fish sauce, sugar, lime juice, chillies, a little salt and pepper and finally the drained noodles. Stir-fry for 3–4 minutes. Turn onto a large platter and sprinkle the garnishes on top. Serve at once, or let it cool and serve at room temperature.

For Ken Hom's guide to ingredients, go to
www.mykitchentable.co.uk/authors/KenHom/ingredients

Ginger Fish Soup

One of the best Chinese techniques for cooking delicate foods such as fish is to steep them, that is, to add the fish pieces to hot broth and turn the heat off. The gentle heat of the broth cooks the fish perfectly – resulting in moist and flavourful fish – without overcooking it or drying it out. In this recipe, I use the technique to make an elegant fish soup.

Step one Remove the skins from the fish and then cut the fillets into pieces about 5cm (2in) square and set aside. If you're using fresh tomatoes, cut them into 2.5cm (1in) cubes. If you're using tinned tomatoes, chop them into small chunks. Pour the stock into a wok or large pan and bring it to a simmer. Add the rice wine or sherry, ginger, 2 teaspoons of salt and 1 teaspoon of pepper and simmer for 5 minutes.

Step two Add the fish, remove the pan from the heat and let it sit for 5 minutes or just until the fish turns white. Using a slotted spoon, transfer the fish to individual bowls or a soup tureen.

Step three Stir the spring onions, coriander, tomatoes, chives and oil into the soup. Ladle the soup over the fish and serve staight away.

Serves 2–4

450g (1lb) fresh, flat, white fish fillets, such as plaice or sole

225g (8oz) tomatoes, pceled and de-seeded if fresh, drained if tinned

1.2 litres (2 pints) home-made or good-quality bought fish stock or chicken stock

2 tsp Shaoxing rice wine or dry sherry

2 tsp finely shredded fresh root ginger

2 tbsp finely chopped spring onions

1 tbsp finely chopped fresh coriander

1 tbsp finely snipped fresh chives

1 tbsp extra-virgin olive oil

salt and pepper

Oxtail Wonton Soup

This soup does require a lengthy period of simmering to tenderise the oxtail – the rich flavour is worth it in the end though.

Serves 4–6 (makes about 30 wontons)

750g (1¾lb) oxtail, jointed

2.75 litres (5 pints) home-made or good-quality bought chicken stock

1 tsp sesame oil

1½ tbsp capers, rinsed and chopped

1 tbsp Dijon mustard

1 tsp finely chopped lemon zest

1½ tsp dark soy sauce

1½ tbsp finely snipped fresh chives

1 tbsp finely chopped fresh chervil

2 tbsp finely chopped shallots, squeezed dry

1 tbsp finely chopped fresh coriander

1 tbsp finely chopped spring onions

250g (9oz) wonton skins

1½ tbsp finely snipped fresh chives, to garnish

salt and pepper

Step one Bring a large pan of water to the boil and put in the oxtail pieces to cook for 15 minutes. Remove and drain well. Bring 2.25 litres (4 pints) of the stock to a simmer in a very large pan, add the oxtail, cover and simmer for 3 hours or until the oxtail is very tender. Skim the surface from time to time, removing any impurities. Cool thoroughly and remove all surface fat. Keep the stock for the soup – you should have about 1.2 litres (2 pints).

Step two To make the wonton filling, remove all the meat from the bones and discard the bones. Finely chop the meat and combine it with the sesame oil, capers, mustard, lemon zest, soy sauce, chives, chervil, shallots, coriander, spring onions, ½ teaspoon of salt and ¼ teaspoon of pepper. Mix well.

Step three When you are ready to stuff the wontons, put 1 tablespoon of the filling in the centre of the first wonton skin. Dampen the edges with a little water and bring up the sides of the skin around the filling. Pinch the edges together at the top so that the wonton is sealed. It should look like a small, filled bag. Repeat the process until all the filling has been used.

Step four Reheat the soup stock and add the remainder of the chicken stock. Season with salt and pepper to taste.

Step five In another pan, bring a large pan of salted water to the boil and put in the wontons to poach for 1 minute, or until they float to the top (you may have to do this in batches). Remove them immediately and transfer to individual flat soup plates. Ladle a small amount of the stock into each soup plate, garnish with chives and serve at once.

Cantonese Egg Flower Soup

This easy soup is found in almost every Chinese restaurant and no wonder since it's tasty and fantastically exotic. Lightly beaten egg lies flat on the surface of the soup like lilies on a pond. This effect is created by gently guiding the egg over the soup in strands instead of dropping the mixture in all at once, which would cause it to lump together. The egg mixture slightly thickens the soup, which nonetheless remains very light.

Step one Put the egg and sesame oil in a small jug or bowl, mix with a fork and set aside. Put the stock in a pot and bring to a simmer. Add the sugar, soy sauce and 1 teaspoon of salt and stir to mix them in well. Stir in the white part of the spring onions. Next add the egg mixture in a very slow, thin stream.

Step two Using chopsticks or a fork, pull the egg slowly into strands. I find that stirring the egg in a figure of eight works quite well. Garnish with the green spring onion tops.

Serves 4

1 egg, lightly beaten

2 tsp sesame oil

1.2 litres (2 pints) home-made or good-quality bought chicken stock

1 tsp sugar

1 tbsp light soy sauce

3 tbsp finely shredded spring onions, white part only

3 tbsp finely shredded green spring onion tops, to garnish

salt

Sweetcorn and Crab Soup

This popular Chinese soup has captivated Western diners. My mother often made it using fresh sweetcorn. For convenience, tinned or frozen corn may be substituted but I think my mother's recipe is superior.

Serves 4

450g (1lb) corn on the cob, or 275g (10oz) tinned or frozen sweetcorn

1 egg white

1 tsp sesame oil

1.2 litres (2 pints) home-made or good-quality bought fish stock

1 tbsp Shaoxing rice wine or dry sherry

1 tbsp light soy sauce

2 tsp finely chopped fresh root ginger

1 tsp sugar

2 tsp cornflour, blended with 2 tsp water

225g (8oz) fresh or frozen crabmeat

2 tbsp finely chopped spring onions, to garnish

salt and white pepper

Step one If you are using fresh corn, pull back the husks, wash the cobs and then remove the kernels with a sharp knife or cleaver. You should end up with about 275g (10oz) corn.

Step two Mix the egg white and sesame oil together in a small jug or bowl and set aside. Bring the stock to the boil in a large pot and add the corn. Simmer for 5 minutes, uncovered, then add the rice wine or sherry, light soy sauce, ginger, sugar, cornflour mixture, 1 teaspoon of salt and ½ teaspoon of white pepper. Bring back to the boil, then lower the heat to a simmer. Add the crabmeat.

Step three Immediately afterwards, slowly pour in the egg white mixture in a steady stream, stirring all the time. Transfer the soup to a tureen or individual bowls and garnish with the spring onions.

Cantonese Wonton Soup

This is one of the most popular soups in food stalls in southern China.

Step one For the filling, put the prawns and pork in a large bowl, add 1 teaspoon of salt and ½ teaspoon of pepper and mix well, either by kneading with your hand or stirring thoroughly with a wooden spoon.

Step two Add all the other filling ingredients and mix thoroughly. Cover the bowl with clingfilm and chill for at least 20 minutes.

Step three To stuff the wontons, put 1 tablespoon of the filling in the centre of each wonton skin. Dampen the edges with a little water and bring them up around the filling. Pinch the edges together at the top so that the wonton is sealed; it should look like a small, filled bag.

Step four Put the stock, soy sauce and sesame oil in a large pot and bring to a simmer. Meanwhile, bring a large pan of salted water to the boil and put in the wontons to poach, in batches, for 1 minute or until they float to the top.

Step five Remove the wontons immediately and transfer them to the pot of stock. (Poaching them first results in a cleaner-tasting broth.) Simmer them in the stock for 2 minutes. Transfer to a soup tureen or individual bowls, garnish with the spring onion tops and serve immediately.

Serves 4

225g (8oz) wonton skins, thawed if necessary

1.2 litres (2 pints) home-made or good-quality bought chicken stock

1 tbsp light soy sauce

1 tsp sesame oil

a handful of chopped green spring onion tops, to garnish

for the filling

225g (8oz) raw prawns, peeled, de-veined and coarsely chopped

225g (8oz) minced fatty pork

1½ tbsp light soy sauce

3 tbsp finely chopped spring onions (white part only)

2 tsp finely chopped fresh root ginger

1 tbsp Shaoxing rice wine or dry sherry

1 tsp sugar

2 tsp sesame oil

1 egg white, lightly beaten

salt and pepper

Spicy Hot and Sour Soup

This northern and western Chinese soup has become quite popular in the West because it is a hearty dish, suited to cold climates.

Serves 4

1.2 litres (2 pints) home-made or good-quality bought chicken stock

100g (4oz) lean pork

25g (1oz) Chinese dried mushrooms

15g (½oz) dried tree fungus or wood ear fungus

225g (8oz) fresh firm bean curd, drained

2 eggs, beaten with pinch of salt

4 tsp sesame oil

1½ tbsp light soy sauce

1 tbsp dark soy sauce

6 tbsp Chinese white rice vinegar

2 tsp chilli oil

2 tbsp fresh coriander

salt and white pepper

for the marinade

1 tsp light soy sauce

1 tsp Shaoxing rice wine or dry sherry

½ tsp sesame oil

½ tsp cornflour

pinch of salt

pinch of sugar

Step one Bring the stock to a simmer in a large pot and add 2 teaspoons of salt. Meanwhile, finely shred the pork and combine it with the marinade ingredients. Mix well and set aside.

Step two Soak the mushrooms and the tree or wood ear fungus until soft, then dry them and remove the stems. Finely shred the remaining caps along with the bean curd and set aside. In a small bowl, combine the eggs with 2 teaspoons of the sesame oil. Stir the pork into the stock and simmer for 1 minute. Then add the mushrooms and bean curd and simmer for a further 2 minutes.

Step three Pour in the egg mixture in a slow, thin, steady stream. Using chopsticks or a fork, pull the egg slowly into strands.

Step four Remove the soup from the heat, and add the soy sauces, vinegar and 1 teaspoon of white pepper. Give the soup a good stir, then stir in the remaining sesame oil, plus the chilli oil. Chop the coriander and stir this in as well. Ladle into a soup tureen or individual bowls and serve straight away.

Tasty Fried Prawns

This Thai dish, *ghoong thod*, is characteristically elegant and complex in taste. The secret is marinating the prawns. They are then surprisingly simple to cook, as they are deep-fried very quickly.

Step one Briefly process all the marinade ingredients together with 2 teaspoons of water in a blender or food-processor. Pour the marinade over the prawns and mix well. Chill for at least 2 hours.

Step two Drain the marinade from the prawns, scraping off any bits; discard the marinade. Dust the prawns with flour, shaking off any excess.

Step three Heat a wok or large frying pan over a high heat and add the oil. When it is very hot and slightly smoking, add a handful of prawns and deep-fry for 3 minutes, until golden and crisp. If the oil gets too hot, reduce the heat slightly. Drain the prawns well on kitchen paper and fry the remaining prawns. Serve immediately.

Serves 4

450g (1lb) raw prawns, shelled and de-veined

plain flour, for dusting

600ml (1 pint) vegetable oil, for deep-frying

for the marinade

3 dried red chillies, chopped

2 tbsp chopped shallots

3 tbsp coarsely chopped garlic

2 tbsp finely chopped fresh galangal or fresh root ginger

3 tbsp chopped coriander root or coriander stalks

1 tbsp fish sauce (nam pla)

1 tbsp lime juice

50ml (2fl oz) tinned coconut milk

Have you made this recipe? Tell us what you think at
www.mykitchentable.co.uk/blog

Two-minute Coconut Prawn Starter

My first experience with this delicious starter was at the Lemon Grass Restaurant in Bangkok. I was determined to find out how it was made and was pleased to learn how quick and easy it is. The chefs used coconut milk made from scratch but I have found tinned coconut milk perfectly acceptable. Imagine my surprise when I was told it was made in the microwave! Truly an East-meets-West dish.

Serves 4

225g (8oz) large raw prawns (about 8)

2 tsp sugar

3 tbsp lime juice

4 tbsp tinned coconut milk

salt and pepper

to garnish

3 tbsp finely sliced shallots

2 small fresh red Thai chillies, coarsely chopped

Step one Peel the prawns and discard the shells. Using a small, sharp knife, remove the fine digestive cords. Rinse the prawns in cold water with 1 tablespoon of salt. Drain and repeat. Rinse well and pat dry with kitchen paper.

Step two Combine the prawns with the sugar and lime juice, and season with 1 teaspoon of salt and some pepper. Mix well. Arrange the prawns on a small platter. Pour the coconut milk over the prawns. Microwave at full power for 2 minutes. If you don't have a microwave, set up a steamer or put a rack in a wok or deep pan and pour in 5cm (2in) of water.

Step three Bring the water to the boil or a high heat and lower the prawns into the steamer or onto the rack. Steam for 3–4 minutes, while heating the coconut milk in a separate pan.

Step four Remove the prawns, pour over the coconut milk if you have steamed them, garnish with shallots and chillies and serve immediately.

Grilled Indonesian Prawn Skewers

One of the pleasures of walking through the streets of Jakarta is smelling the wafting aromas of the various grilled foods being cooked. This dish is probably one of my favourites – juicy, succulent prawns that have been marinated and then cooked quickly on a barbecue or hot grill. The smoky chargrilled taste complements the delicious prawns so well. This dish takes only minutes to cook.

Step one Soak 12 bamboo skewers in cold water for 15 minutes. Meanwhile, combine all the marinade ingredients in a large bowl, season with 1 teaspoon of salt and ½ teaspoon of pepper and mix well.

Step two Add the prawns to the marinade and mix well. Cover with clingfilm and leave to marinate in the fridge for at least 1 hour.

Step three When you are ready to barbecue the prawns, remove them from the marinade and thread one or two onto each bamboo skewer. Reserve the marinade.

Step four Prepare a barbecue or preheat a ridged chargrill pan or the oven grill. When the charcoal is ash white or the grill is very hot, grill the prawn skewers for 2–3 minutes on each side, until they are cooked through.

Step five Pour the marinade into a small pan and simmer for 2 minutes. Arrange the prawn skewers on a warm platter and serve immediately, accompanied by the sauce.

Serves 4–6

450g (1lb) raw prawns, shelled and de-veined

for the marinade

100ml (4fl oz) tinned coconut milk

1 tbsp fish sauce (nam pla)

3 tbsp lime juice

2 tbsp finely chopped garlic

1 tsp finely chopped lime zest

2 small, fresh red chillies, de-seeded and chopped

2 tsp sugar

1 tsp shrimp paste

salt and pepper

Malaysian Prawn Fritters

I remember the first time I had these fritters at a roadside restaurant in Kuala Lumpur. Quickly fried and served immediately, they were absolutely divine. Then I discovered how easy they were to make. They make a wonderful first course with salad, or serve with drinks.

Serves 4, makes about 20 fritters

450g (1lb) raw prawns, shelled and de-veined

225g (8oz) fresh beansprouts, rinsed

120g (4½ oz) plain flour

2 tsp baking powder

2 small, fresh red chillies, de-seeded and finely chopped

1 tsp ground coriander

½ tsp ground turmeric

2 tbsp finely chopped spring onions

2 tbsp finely chopped fresh coriander

2 eggs, beaten

400ml (14fl oz) oil, preferably ground nut, for deep-frying

salt and pepper

Step one Finely chop half the prawns. Combine the chopped prawns with the beansprouts, flour, baking powder, chillies, ground coriander, turmeric, spring onions, fresh coriander, eggs, 1 teaspoon of salt and a little pepper. Mix well.

Step two Take a dessertspoonful of the chopped mixture, place one whole prawn on top and press it into the mixture so that the prawn is set in. Continue until you have used up all the mixture and whole prawns.

Step three Heat the oil in a deep fryer or a large wok. Deep-fry the fritters, a few at a time, for 2–3 minutes, until they are golden brown. Drain them on kitchen paper and serve at once.

Crackling Rice-paper-wrapped Fish

This dish is a great example of typical Fusion cooking. I use rice paper (a very Asian ingredient) to wrap cod (a very European fish), and season it at the same time with fresh Asian and Western herbs, and a touch of Madras curry powder. It is surprisingly easy to make and the results are a delightful crackling and stunning-looking appetiser that will surely impress your family, friends and guests. You can also use halibut or sea bass instead of cod.

Serves 4

450g (1lb) boneless skinless cod, halibut or sea bass

2 tsp Madras curry powder

2 tbsp plain flour

1 packet dried rice paper in 22cm (8½ in) rounds

8 fresh coriander leaves

3 tbsp snipped fresh chives

2 tbsp ground nut oil

extra-virgin olive oil, to serve

salt and pepper

Step one Divide the fish into four equal pieces, about 7.5 x 7.5cm (3 x 3in). Combine the curry powder with 1 teaspoon of salt and ½ teaspoon of pepper. Sprinkle the mixture evenly over the fish pieces.

Step two Make the sealing mixture by mixing the flour with 2 tablespoons of water. Fill a large bowl with hot water and dip one of the rice paper rounds into the water to soften. This will take but a few seconds. Remove and drain on a clean tea towel.

Step three In the centre of the round, layer two coriander leaves, a piece of fish and 2 teaspoons of chives on top. Fold the first edge over the ingredients, then fold in the sides. Fold the remaining side over and seal with a little flour-paste mixture to secure the parcel. Repeat for the other three rounds to form four parcels.

Step four Heat a large, heavy frying pan over a high heat until it is hot; then add the ground nut oil. When the oil is hot, add the four parcels and pan-fry on the seamless side for about 3 minutes or until golden brown. Turn over to the other side and continue to cook until golden brown.

Step five Now arrange the packages on a platter. Drizzle with olive oil and serve at once.

Dim Sum-style Pork Dumplings

Chinese restaurant diners usually enjoy discovering these teahouse treats, which have always been a favourite of the southern Chinese.

Makes about 40 dumplings

1 packet of wonton skins (about 40), thawed if necessary

a little vegetable oil

for the filling

100g (4oz) fresh or tinned water chestnuts, peeled if fresh, finely chopped

100g (4oz) raw prawns, shelled, de-veined and coarsely chopped

350g (12oz) minced fatty pork

2 tbsp finely chopped Parma ham or lean smoked bacon

1 tbsp light soy sauce

1 tsp dark soy sauce

1 tbsp Shaoxing rice wine or dry sherry

3 tbsp finely chopped spring onions

2 tsp finely chopped fresh root ginger

2 tsp sesame oil

1 egg white, lightly beaten

2 tsp sugar

salt and pepper

Step one To make the filling, put all the ingredients in a bowl, season with 1 teaspoon of salt and ½ teaspoon of pepper and mix together thoroughly. Place a portion of the filling on each wonton skin. Bring up the sides and press them around the filling mixture. Tap the dumpling on the bottom to make a flat base. The top should be wide open, exposing the filling.

Step two Set up a steamer or put a rack inside a wok or large, deep pot. Pour in about 5cm (2in) of water and bring to the boil. Oil the rack, or the inside of the steamer, to prevent the dumplings from sticking. Put the dumplings on it (you may have to cook them in several batches).

Step three Cover the pot tightly, turn the heat to low and steam gently for about 20 minutes. To save time, use a larger steamer to cook bigger batches. Serve the dumplings hot; they can be reheated if necessary by steaming gently for a few minutes.

For step-by-step photographs of this recipe, go to
www.mykitchentable.co.uk/recipes/dimsumpork

Asian-flavoured Aubergine Crostini

Aubergine dips are popular in Mediterranean countries. During one of my many East–West vegetarian cookery promotions at the famed Oriental Hotel in Bangkok, I offered this spicy dip. Though it takes a little time to prepare, it proved to be quite popular.

Step one Preheat the oven to 240°C/475°F/gas 9. If you are using Chinese aubergines, roast them for 20 minutes; if you are using ordinary large aubergines, roast them for about 30–40 minutes, or until they are soft and cooked through.

Step two Halfway through the roasting, add the garlic and tomatoes. Allow them to cool and then peel the aubergines, tomatoes and garlic. Put them in a colander and let them drain for 30 minutes. This procedure can be done a few hours in advance, if need be.

Step three Combine the aubergines, tomatoes and garlic in a food-processor with the remainder of the ingredients, except the bread. Season with ¼ teaspoon each of salt and pepper and process until well blended. Toast the French bread slices and serve straight away.

Serves 4–6

900g (2lb) Chinese or ordinary aubergines

3 garlic cloves

225g (8oz) fresh tomatoes

1½ tbsp ground nut oil

1 onion, finely chopped

1 tbsp finely chopped fresh root ginger

2 tbsp finely chopped fresh coriander

2 tbsp finely chopped spring onions

2 tsp finely chopped orange zest

2 tsp chilli bean sauce

1 tsp light soy sauce

2 tbsp black rice vinegar

1 tsp sesame oil

1 tbsp sesame seeds, toasted

1 tsp sugar

French bread, thinly sliced diagonally

salt and pepper

Crispy Corn Cakes

These make a wonderfully enticing starter – a savoury mixture of corn and pork fried to crispy morsels. To speed things up when you are cooking for a dinner party, you could partially fry the corn cakes in advance and then plunge them into hot oil again just before serving. Their Thai name is *tod mun khao phod*.

Serves 4–6

450g (1lb) fresh corn on the cob, or 275g (10oz) tinned sweetcorn

175g (6oz) minced fatty pork

2 tbsp finely chopped fresh coriander

2 tbsp finely chopped garlic

2 tbsp fish sauce (nam pla)

1 tsp sugar

1 tbsp cornflour

2 eggs, beaten

600ml (1 pint) vegetable oil, for deep-frying

white pepper

to garnish

a handful of fresh coriander sprigs

1 small cucumber, peeled and thinly sliced

Step one If using corn on the cob, strip off the husks and the silk and cut off the kernels with a sharp knife or cleaver. You should end up with about 275g (10oz). If you are using tinned corn, drain it well.

Step two Put half of the corn in a blender, add all the remaining ingredients except the oil, season with ½ teaspoon of white pepper and blend to a purée. Pour this mixture into a bowl and stir in the remainder of the corn.

Step three Heat a wok or large frying pan over a high heat and add the oil. When it is very hot and slightly smoking, pour in a small ladleful of the corn mixture. Repeat until the wok is full. Reduce the heat to low and cook for 1–2 minutes, until the fritters are brown underneath, then turn them over and fry the other side.

Step four Remove the fritters from the wok with a slotted spoon and drain on kitchen paper. Keep them warm while you cook the remaining fritters. Arrange on a warm platter, garnish with the coriander and sliced cucumber and serve at once.

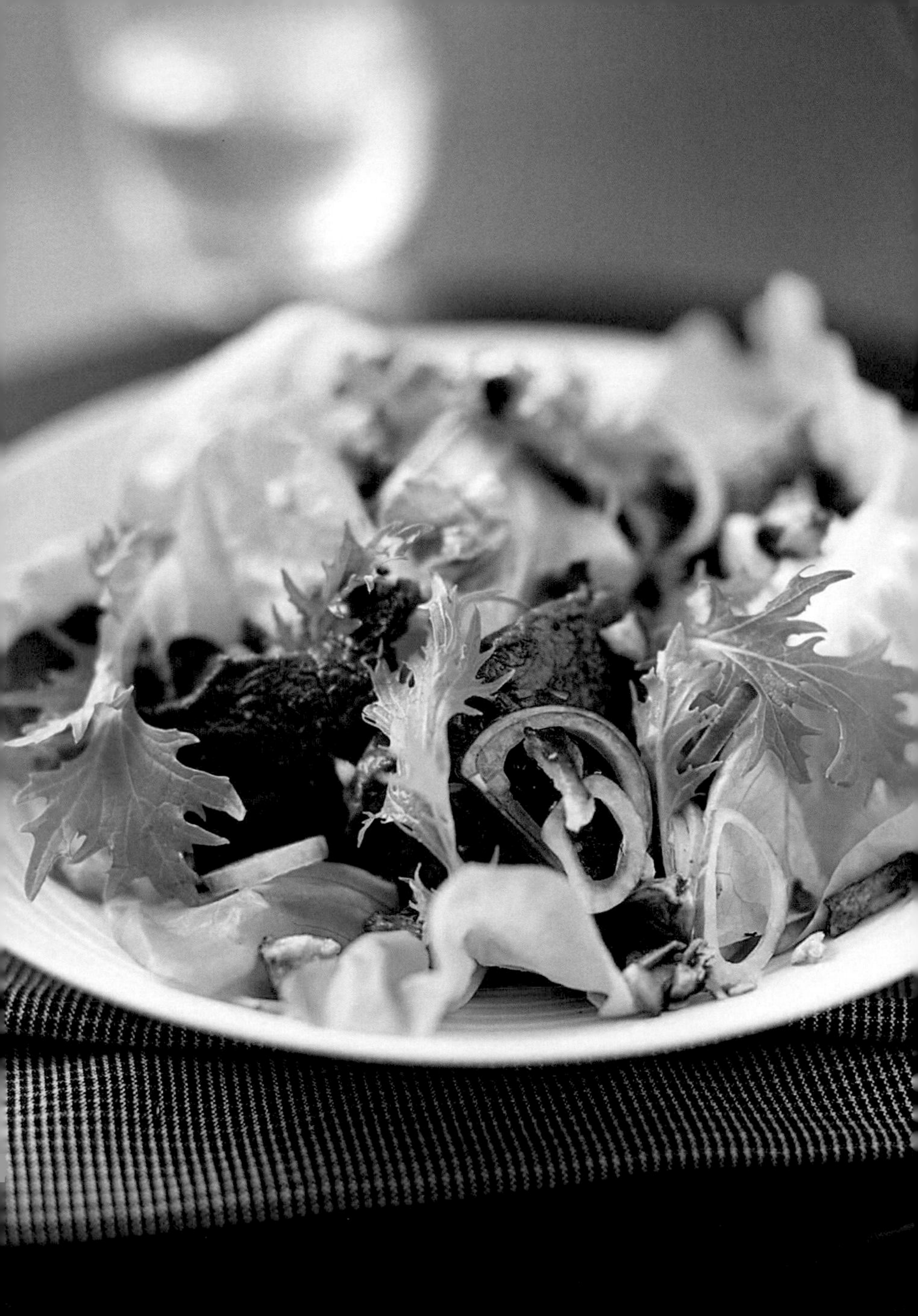

Warm Vietnamese Beef Salad

This is one of my favourite Vietnamese dishes. It has a clean, light flavour, with the stir-fried beef paired with a freshly dressed green salad that is typical of dishes served in tropical Vietnam. Although it is often served as a starter, I find it equally delicious as a main course in hot weather; simply double the quantities or add more salad.

Serves 4–6

450g (1lb) lean, tender beef fillet

1 tbsp fish sauce
(nam pla)

1 tbsp light soy sauce

1 tsp sugar

3 tbsp oil, preferably ground nut oil

5 tbsp coarsely chopped garlic

225g (8oz) soft lettuce leaves

for the dressing

3 tbsp white rice vinegar

1 tbsp finely chopped garlic

2 tsp sesame oil

3 tbsp oil, preferably ground nut oil

6 tbsp finely sliced shallots

salt and pepper

Step one First make the dressing. In a large salad bowl, combine the vinegar, garlic and some salt and pepper. Gradually beat in the sesame and ground nut oils, then stir in the shallots and set aside until needed.

Step two Cut the beef into slices 5cm (2in) long and 5mm (¼in) thick, slicing against the grain of the meat. Put the beef into a bowl together with the fish sauce, soy sauce, sugar and some black pepper. Mix well and then leave to marinate for about 20 minutes.

Step three Heat a wok or large frying pan over a high heat until it is very hot. Add the oil and, when it is hot, add the garlic and stir-fry for 20 seconds, until golden brown. Remove with a slotted spoon and drain on kitchen paper.

Step four Reheat the oil and, when it is very hot and slightly smoking, add the beef to the wok and stir-fry for 2 minutes, until it is barely cooked. Remove it and leave to drain in a colander or sieve.

Step five Add the greens to the dressing in the salad bowl and toss thoroughly. Arrange on a serving platter, garnish with the browned garlic and top with the warm beef. Serve at once.

Spicy Papaya Salad

In hot and humid Thailand, room-temperature salads such as this *som tam* often accompany meals. Their spicy coolness makes them the perfect balance for heavier dishes and the bonus is that they can be prepared ahead of time. Green papaya works best here because it is slightly tart, with the crispness of a fresh apple. You will find the crunchy texture and spicy flavours of this salad quite addictive. Serve as a starter or an accompaniment to a main course.

Serves 4

1 green, unripe papaya

2 small, fresh red Thai chillies, de-seeded and chopped

2 garlic cloves, crushed

2 tbsp chopped shallots

2 tbsp lime juice

1 tbsp fish sauce (nam pla)

1 tbsp sugar

salt

to garnish

3–4 tbsp crushed roasted peanuts

2 small, fresh red Thai chillies, de-seeded and sliced (optional)

Step one Peel the papaya and cut it in half lengthways. Remove the seeds and finely shred the flesh.

Step two Put the chillies, garlic, shallots and ½ teaspoon of salt in a mortar and pestle. Add a quarter of the shredded papaya and pound gently until it is slightly softened (if you don't have a mortar and pestle, simply stir the ingredients together or crush them against the side of a bowl with a wooden spoon). Continue to add more of the shredded papaya until it is used up.

Step three Add the lime juice, fish sauce and sugar. Toss carefully and arrange on a platter. Garnish with the crushed peanuts and the sliced chillies, if using.

Indonesian Vegetable Salad

This is a delightful cooked vegetarian salad, dressed with a bold peanut sauce. Considered a national dish in Indonesia, it makes the perfect antidote to the hot, humid weather of Java. I find it makes a good light first course for a dinner party, or it can be served as a meal in itself.

Step one First make the peanut sauce. Finely chop the garlic and de-seed and chop the chillies. Combine all of the ingredients except the peanuts in a blender along with 5 tablespoons of water and process thoroughly. Pour into a small bowl and leave to stand for at least 10 minutes before using (the sauce can be prepared several hours in advance, if necessary).

Step two Bring a large pan of salted water to the boil and put in the carrots, broccoli, cauliflower and green beans to cook for 3 minutes, then add the beansprouts and cook for 1 minute. Drain the vegetables, place in a warm bowl and season with a little salt and pepper.

Step three Heat a wok then add the ground nut oil. When the oil is hot, toss in the sliced shallots and fry slowly until crisp and brown (watch them carefully so they don't burn). Remove immediately with a slotted spoon and drain on kitchen paper.

Step four Just before serving, crush the roasted peanuts and stir them into the peanut sauce. Drizzle the sauce over the vegetables and mix well, then transfer to a serving platter. Garnish with the fried shallots, then shell the eggs, cut them into quarters and put them on top of the salad. Arrange the remainder of the garnishes on top and serve at once.

Serves 4

225g (8oz) carrots, peeled and thinly sliced

100g (4oz) small broccoli florets

100g (4oz) small cauliflower florets

100g (4oz) green beans, trimmed

100g (4oz) fresh beansprouts, rinsed

3 tbsp ground nut oil

5 shallots, sliced

salt and pepper

for the peanut sauce

1 tbsp garlic

1–2 fresh red chillies

2 tbsp fish sauce (nam pla)

2 tbsp lemon juice

1 tbsp sugar

3 tbsp roasted peanuts, crushed

to garnish

2 eggs, hard-boiled for 10–12 minutes

prawn crackers

1 small cucumber, thinly sliced

Cold Bean Curd Salad

The secret of this dish is the use of soft, silky Japanese bean curd, an ingredient that ensures success. This delicate version of bean curd is akin to a semi-soft pudding, but what makes it work is its congeniality, its ability to take on ambient aromas and flavours. Definitely a Fusion recipe to try.

Serves 4

450g (1lb) silky Japanese bean curd

6 tbsp chopped fresh coriander

6 tbsp chopped spring onion tops

3 tbsp extra-virgin olive oil

salt and pepper

Step one Allow the bean curd to drain for 10 minutes. Place it on a platter and sprinkle evenly with the coriander, spring onions, 1 teaspoon of salt and ½ teaspoon of pepper. Drizzle with olive oil and serve at once.

Asian-flavoured aubergine
crostini
194–5
asparagus
in black bean sauce 110–11
savoury beef with 68–9
aubergines
Asian-flavoured crostini
194–5
rich, with tomato and basil
130–1
stir-fried Thai green
chicken with 26–7
bean curd salad, cold 204–5
beef
fragrant, with peppers
58–9
Indonesian fried 142–3
Malaysian-style satay 64–5
Mussaman-style curry 66–7
savoury, with asparagus
68–9
stir–fried, with oyster
sauce 62–3
Vietnamese–style lemon
grass 60–1
warm Vietnamese salad
198–9
with peppercorns 56–7
black bean sauce
asparagus in 110–11
Cantonese crab with 96–7
prawns and scallops in
black bean and tomato
butter sauce 80–1
stir-fried chicken with
14–15
stir-fried fish with 88–9
broad beans with red curry
116–17
broccoli
delectable chicken 34–5
Hong Kong-style, and baby
corn 112–13
stir-fried 102–3
Cantonese crab with black
bean sauce 96–7
Cantonese egg flower soup
174–5

Cantonese wonton soup
178–9
carrots, ginger and garlic
114–15
cashews, stir-fried chilli
pork with 42–3
chicken
Chinese curry 20–1
chow mein 152–3
classic lemon 18–19
classic Vietnamese lemon
grass 30–1
delectable broccoli 34–5
fried rice with basil 138–9
green curry 22–3
Indonesian-style, with
vegetables 12–13
red curry 24–5
shredded, with sesame
seeds 8–9
spicy, with peanuts 16–17
stir-fried Thai green curry
with aubergines 26–7
stir-fried with black bean
sauce 14–15
stir-fried with grilled
peppers 6–7
stir-fried, with Chinese
and button mushrooms 28–9
Thai-style 36–7
with chillies and basil
10–11
Wolfgang Puck's stir-fried,
with garlic and fresh
coriander 32–3
Chinese chicken curry 20–1
chow mein 152–3
crab
and sweetcorn soup 176–7
Cantonese, with black bean
sauce 96–7
crostini, Asian-flavoured
aubergine 194–5
curry
broad beans with red
116–17
Chinese chicken 20–1
fragrant prawn 82–3
green chicken 22–3

green Thai mussels 98–9
Mussaman-style beef 66–7
red chicken 24–5
rice noodles with
vegetables 160–1
stir-fried pasta with
orange and 166–7
stir-fried Thai green
chicken 26–7
duck, Thai-style 38–9
egg noodles
chow mein 152–3
spicy Sechuan 156–7
eggs
Cantonese egg flower soup
174–5
egg-fried rice 136–5
fish
crackling
rice-paper-wrapped 190–1
ginger, soup 170–1
stir-fried, with black bean
sauce 88–9
ginger fish soup 170–1
green beans
bright pepper and, stir-fry
118–19
Indonesian-style sambal
124–5
green chicken curry 22–3
Hong Kong-style broccoli and
baby corn 112–13
Indonesian fried rice 142–3
Indonesian-style green bean
sambal 124–5
Indonesian vegetable salad
202–3
lamb, spicy orange 70–1
lemon
classic lemon chicken 18–19
salmon with 90–1
lemon grass
classic Vietnamese chicken
30–1
Vietnamese-style beef 60–1
Malaysian-style beef satay
64–5
mangetout
cloud ears stir-fried with